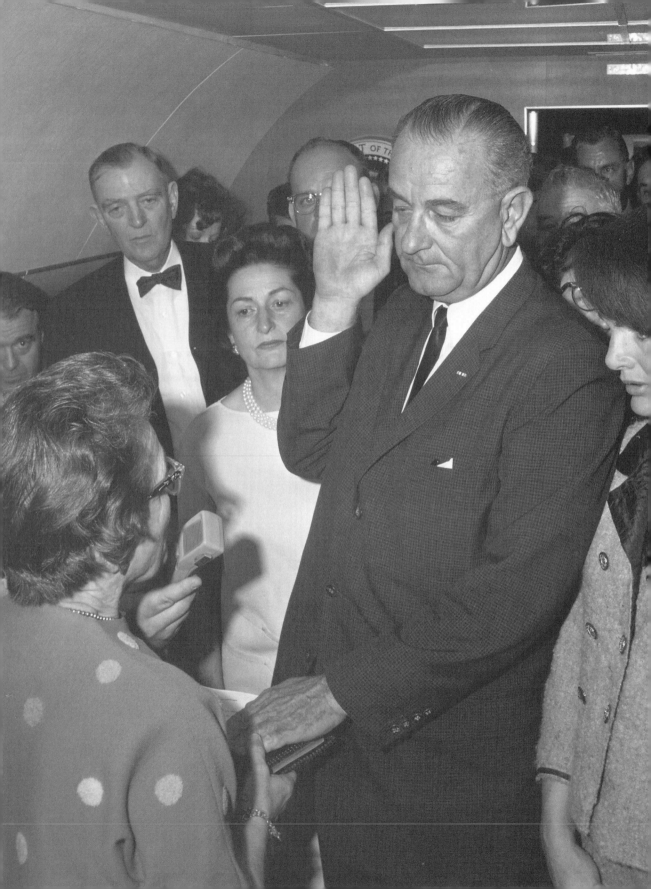

Religion in American Life

JON BUTLER & HARRY S. STOUT
GENERAL EDITORS

Church and State in America

Second Edition

Edwin S. Gaustad

OXFORD UNIVERSITY PRESS
New York • Oxford

Introduction

JON BUTLER & HARRY S. STOUT, GENERAL EDITORS

The issue of church and state is one of the most important and pressing matters we face as a nation. Before the Revolution, many colonial governments supported "established" churches that enjoyed special powers and privileges denied to others. With independence and creation of the American republic, a new concept of church and state appeared: the idea of religious liberty and the separation of church and state. This concept would unleash unprecedented powers in terms of religious innovation and liberty of conscience among generations of Americans and, at the same time, would pose unprecedented problems in defining the "line" or "wall" that separated the realm of government and public life from the realm of religion and individual conscience.

One place that these issues are debated is the U.S. Supreme Court. In the 20th century there has been an increasing number of church and state cases that test First Amendment guarantees of freedom of religion. Indeed, there have been more cases interpreting the First Amendment in the second half of the 20th century than in all earlier periods of American history combined.

Yet the Supreme Court is only the last stop in this complex and endlessly interesting story. In fact, issues of church and state have emerged in cities, towns, and neighborhoods ever since the creation of the American republic. Today they are often seen most dramatically in our nation's schools. Should prayers be allowed in public schools? Should the Bible be

verend Jacob Duché
ads the 1774 Continental
ongress in prayer. The
adition of opening
ongressional sessions
ith an invocation dates
om this time.

taught as literature? Can choral groups sing Christmas carols? These are just a few of the questions that touch people's lives directly and grow out of a separation of church and state. In this volume, one of the most distinguished scholars of American religious history tells the fascinating story of church and state from the colonial period, through the Revolution and its "grand experiment" in religious liberty, right up to the present. The problems he raises are important and affect students and parents alike. In fact, today's young people will be writing new chapters in this history as they face the issues of church and state in their own lives.

This book is part of a unique 17-volume series that explores the evolution, character, and dynamics of religion in American life from 1500 to the end of the 20th century. It is impossible to capture the flavor and character of the American experience without understanding the connections between secular activities and religion. Spirituality stood at the center of Native American societies before European colonization and has continued to do so long after. Religion—and the freedom to express it—motivated milllions of immigrants to come to America from remarkably different cultures, and the exposure to new ideas and ways of living shaped their experience. It also fueled tension among different ethnic and racial groups in America and, regretfully, accounted for difficult episodes of bigotry in American society. Religion urged Americans to expand the nation—first within the continental United States, then through overseas conquests and missionary work—and has had a profound influence on American politics, from the era of the Puritans to the present. Finally, religion contributes to the extraordinary diversity that has, for four centuries, made the United States one of the world's most dynamic societies.

The Religion in American Life series explores the historical traditions that have made religious freedom and spiritual exploration central features of American society. It emphasizes the experience of religion in America—what men and women have understood by religion, how it has affected politics and society, and how Americans have used it to shape their daily lives.

Preface

n 1651 Boston authorities laid 30 lashes on the bare back of a Baptist from Rhode Island who dared to invade their territory. In 1654 the Dutch Governor of New York (then New Amsterdam) required a small group of Jews who tried to settle there to leave promptly for other lands. Also in 1654, a new government in Maryland decreed that "none who profess and exercise the Popish Religion commonly known by the name of the Roman Catholic religion can be protected in this Province." In 1659 the first of four Quakers was hanged in Boston Common. In 1707 a Presbyterian minister was thrown into a New York jail for the crime of preaching his version of the Christian gospel. And in Virginia in 1774 some traveling preachers were imprisoned for declaring their religious opinions. This action so offended 23-year-old James Madison that he cried out against the "diabolical, hell-conceived principle of persecution."

Could all of this have happened in the United States of America? Well, not quite. These events occurred in America, to be sure, but they happened before there was a United States in 1776, or a Constitution in 1789, or a First Amendment in 1791. Jails, fines, floggings, and sentences of exile or death were commonplace before federal guarantees of religious liberty began to take effect. Now, in marked contrast to those earlier days, millions of Americans flock to their respective churches, synagogues, mosques, and other religious gathering places on Fridays, or Saturdays, or Sundays—or any other time that they choose. And the hand of the state is never raised against them.

The U.S. Supreme Court interprets the boundary between church and state. The court's landmark decisions have had tremendous impact on our expression religious liberty.

Of course, it would be too simple a picture to suppose that after 1791 all examples of persecution or bigotry miraculously disappeared. In 1830, for example, a newly founded anti-Catholic weekly dedicated itself to defeat all "Romish corruptions—to maintain the purity and sufficiency of the Holy Scriptures against Monkish Traditions." Four years later, an angry mob in Charlestown, Massachusetts, burned an Ursuline convent to the ground, and 10 years after that rioting gangs in Philadelphia destroyed two Catholic churches and a seminary attached to one of them. In the 1850s, the rise of the Know-Nothing Party revealed a deep-seated hostility to foreigners in general, to Roman Catholics, Jews, and African Americans in particular. In 1887 the American Protective Association was founded for the purpose of denying citizenship to all persons subject to "any ecclesiastical power not created and controlled by American citizens."

America "must remain Protestant," declared the Imperial Wizard of the Ku Klux Klan in 1926. And in 1928, when Alfred E. Smith became the first Roman Catholic to run for the Presidency of the United States, anti-Catholic rhetoric rose to an ever higher pitch. Resentment against and resistance to Roman Catholicism reflected the great growth of that religion in the United States from the middle of the 19th century on. Likewise, resentment against the rapidly increasing Jewish population around the beginning of the 20th century led to more manifestations of anti-Semitism and the imposing of quotas to restrict the number of Jews admitted into major universities or medical schools and to "better" neighborhoods. By 1913 the Jewish community deemed it useful to create the Anti-Defamation League, whose main purpose was to eradicate, or at least reduce, the religious and racial prejudice spreading across the land.

In the 1920s and 1930s, no group suffered more overt hostility and persecution than did America's blacks. That hostility took its ugliest form in the practice of lynching: execution by hanging or other means, without any legal proceeding or evaluation of evidence. Between 1882 and 1927 nearly 5,000 lynchings took place, the majority inflicted on African Americans. By 1940 the number of lynchings had declined dramatically, but prejudice then took other forms, both institutional and personal.

Clearly, in the realm of religious and racial bigotry, the United States has not yet arrived at some bright new dawn. The nation has, however, managed to avoid religious warfare, an especially bloody type of confrontation that continues to afflict so much of the rest of the world.

In place of religious wars, Americans have substituted discussion and debate, a good deal of it gathered under the heading of "church and state." Such terms as church and state can sound strangely abstract and remote: of little interest to hardly anyone. Yet, for a great many of us, what these terms stand for may be surprisingly near at hand and even personal. Church can represent the local synagogue or mosque, no less than the cathedral or the denominational headquarters; it can also include the church camp or festival, the street preacher, or even the Salvation Army Christmas kettle. State refers to any level of government: local, state, or federal. And those entities can touch the school population (among others) in many ways, from offering inoculations against disease to enforcing curfews and granting driving licenses. The apparent remoteness of church and state is only that: an illusion, a phantom. These institutions involve us all, touch us all, and possibly even change us all.

Lynching was one of the most extreme results of religious and racial intolerance in the early 20th century. Church and state issues create a forum to discuss religious diversity and provide alternatives to violence.

So as readers follow the chapters in this book, they might keep in mind that although black-robed justices and marbled courthouses seem far from our daily life, they are not that distant. We need to know about religious and legal institutions and be alert to their limitations as well as their powers. Many people feel passionately about religion; many people feel passionately about politics. But in the midst of all that passion, a democracy depends on the ability of its citizens to inform themselves, to discuss rationally matters of great concern, and to help mold those decisions that frame the future for us all. In that spirit, we need to understand, even to take on those forbidding institutions called church and state, especially where the two seem to collide or where the goals of our society appear to come into conflict.

FOR THE LORD IS OUR DEFENCE AND THE HOLY ONE OF ISRAEL IS OUR KING

THE PILGRIMS ON THE MAYFLOWER

Chapter 1

The Colonies:
Europe in America

When the European colonization of North America began in the 17th century, the Protestant Reformation was barely 100 years old. The new settlers retained vivid and often painful memories of that period of religious turmoil, during which the newly emerging Protestant sects had broken the unity imposed upon Europe by the Roman Catholic Church. In many cases, the colonists' parents and grandparents had actively participated in aspects of the Protestant movement, or of its counterpart, the Catholic Reformation which attempted to hold onto or recapture European lands for the Catholic Church. Sharp shifts in religious views and loyalties precipitated the breakup of empires and kingdoms, and this in turn led to bloody persecutions and even bloodier wars. In other words, religion in those days was not so much a matter for quiet discussion or debate as it was a matter of martyrs and deserters, of muskets and swords, of burning and butchery.

This brutal aspect of much public religion was intensified by the raging fires of nationalism. One was no longer merely a European or an inhabitant of the Holy Roman Empire, as had been the case earlier. Now one was a fervent nationalist, waving the flag of or bearing arms for Spain or France, Holland or Scotland, Portugal or England. And when political loyalties combined with religious passions, the resulting combinations wielded enormous and fearful power.

This mural in the Massachusetts State House depicts the Pilgrims as they first sighted North America on November 9, 1620. The inscription above their heads testifies to their strong religious faith.

In the European settlement of the Americas, Portugal and Spain seized an early lead. And as they planted their respective national flags—Portugal in Brazil, Spain in Mexico and Peru—they also carried the banners of their dominant religious institution: the Roman Catholic Church. Late in the 16th century, English statesmen, clergymen, and even pirates complained that England was falling behind in the race to the so-called New World. They believed that their national flag deserved a place in the Western Hemisphere, as did their special brand of Protestantism: the Church of England, or Anglicanism (later called the Episcopal Church). Queen Elizabeth I, encouraged by the explorer Sir Walter Raleigh and others, gave her royal approval to early colonization efforts in the 1580s, but these did not succeed. When at last a permanent settlement was achieved in 1607, the large territory was called Virginia in honor of Elizabeth, known as the Virgin Queen, and the tiny settlement itself was called Jamestown in honor of the then reigning monarch, James I.

England's colony of Virginia would quite naturally become the home for England's national church. For this was the way of the world in the 17th century. Church and state were partners in maintaining the safety, stability, and moral order of society. The notion that these two fundamental institutions should somehow be separate, functioning independently of each other, was as novel as it was absurd. The leaders of that time knew that one could not survive without the other, and that no great nation, certainly no feeble or struggling young colony, could survive without the steady support of those two powerful arms, the church and the state. This was the European pattern, and the settlers of Virginia brought that fixed idea with them, just as unquestioningly as they brought their clothes and their weapons.

So when Virginia's governors announced laws for the secular order, they decreed laws for the sacred order at the very same time. And those laws were rigid, harsh, and demanding, in accordance with the prevailing spirit of the times. The Church of England would be the colony's official religion, and no other church would be tolerated. Virginia's settlers would attend morning and evening prayer every day and those who "shall often and willfully absent themselves" from these divine services would be punished according to the law. For the first offense, settlers—already living on the edge of starvation—would lose a day's provision of rations. For a second offense, they would be whipped, and for a third, they would be sentenced to serve in the oceangoing galleys for six months. Harsh penalties were also prescribed for those who took the name of God in vain or who spoke "impiously or maliciously against the holy and blessed Trinity."

Of course, such penalties were designed only for troublemakers, outsiders, and extremists. If everyone simply lived, thought, and worshiped in the accepted and approved Anglican way, the sterner face of the law need not show itself. The governor and his council, the pastor and his congregation, could all work together as a team. One could hardly ask where church responsibilities left off and political responsibilities began. The leading laymen of each parish comprised a vestry that supervised education, distributed charity, and kept a record of births and deaths, in addition to caring for the church structure itself. On the civil side, the sheriff collected taxes for the support of the ministry as well as for the judges and the jailers. All worked together in harmony—for a time.

Beginning with the first settlements in the 1610s and 1620s, geography posed problems. In England the churches rose in the middle of the towns, at the center of population and commercial activity. In Virginia there were no towns, only long and narrow plantations spread out along the broad rivers that served as the colony's only highways. In these circumstances, where should one build a church, and how could a widely scattered population gather for worship? The ministers, moreover, had to be imported from England, for Virginia had no way of training or ordaining its own clergy. And because Virginia did not enjoy a great reputation back "home," the colonists often had cause to complain about both the quality and number of the clergy dispatched to them. Then, too,

Queen Elizabeth I was the head of the Anglican Church when the colony of Virginia was founded. The colony was expected to maintain England's religious structure.

Lord Cornbury, of colonial New York, seated in profile, accuses Francis Makemie of preaching without a license. Religious conformity was a goal of the Anglican governors.

some citizens saw the Anglican Church as a preserver of a social class system, its members more interested in horse racing, gambling, and entertainment than in piety and deep devotion. Finally, Anglicanism failed to keep all other denominations outside its own borders.

By the middle of the 18th century, preachers who were not members of the Church of England began arriving in Virginia. These persons, called Dissenters or Nonconformists in England because they did not belong to the National Church or conform to the services of worship as given in the Book of Common Prayer, aroused much clerical resentment in Virginia. A Presbyterian preacher, Samuel Davies, had to obtain a license from the colonial authorities before he was allowed to preach. To make matters worse, Davies wanted to be licensed to preach not just in one particular location, but anywhere in Virginia. A leading Anglican clergyman, William Dawson, protested in 1752 that the Dissenters were never satisfied. "I think it is high time," Dawson asserted, "for the Government to interpose, to give their immodesty a check and to restrain their teachers within the bounds of a parish, lest their insolence should grow to a dangerous height."

Other Dissenters, such as the Baptists and the Methodists, soon joined with the Presbyterians to challenge the religious monopoly that the Anglicans had enjoyed for a century and a half. From the Anglican perspective, Virginia as a royal colony should support, honor, and pre-serve England's established church, free from challenge or competition. From the Dissenters' perspective, England's Act of Toleration, adopted in 1689, should have guaranteed religious toleration in the colonies no less than in the motherland itself. However, this view remained in dispute, not only in Virginia but in all other colonies where Anglicanism thought of itself as the privileged and protected creed.

In New York, for example, the royal governor, Lord Cornbury, had a Presbyterian preacher, Francis Makemie, arrested in 1707 and brought before him for a sharp interrogation, which included the following exchange:

CORNBURY: How dare you take upon [yourself] to Preach in my Government without my License?

MAKEMIE: We have Liberty from an Act of Parliament [of 1689].

CORNBURY: That Law does not extend to the American Plantations, but only to England.

MAKEMIE: My Lord, I humbly conceive, it is not a limited nor Local Act. . .

CORNBURY: That act of Parliament was made against strolling Preachers, and you are such, and shall not preach in my Government.

MAKEMIE: There is not one word, my Lord, mentioned in any part of the Law, against traveling or strolling Preachers, as your excellency is pleased to call them. . . . And it is well known, my Lord, to all that Quakers, who also have Liberty by this Law, have few or no fixed Teachers . . . [they] Travel and Teach over the Plantations, and are not molested.

CORNBURY: I have troubled some of them, and will trouble them more.

Makemie was jailed for a time, but he was soon released when the royal governor was recalled to England. Cornbury's imperious manner helped neither his church nor his nation.

Anglicanism, stronger in Virginia than elsewhere in the colonies, soon spread throughout the southern colonies and into Pennsylvania, New Jersey, and New York. Yet it did not succeed anywhere in keeping all the competition under control. The European ideal of one church in one nation remained the goal, but it was a goal never fully achieved before the

American Revolution. After that revolution, the Anglican dream was swiftly shattered, never to be realized in any of the American states.

The ideal of blending church and state came somewhat closer to realization in New England, where Puritanism (also known as Congregationalism) flourished as the official, tax-supported church. The word *Puritan* referred to the desire of these worshipers to purify the Church of England of lingering elements of Roman Catholicism. They wanted their church to become more thoroughly Protestant, depending only upon the Bible, not tradition, for the nature of worship and the content of theology. The term *Congregational* arose from the Puritans' desire to make each local church or congregation independent, free from the authority of a bishop or a synod that could demand of worshipers what to do or what to believe. But politically each church was not a law unto itself, for the state (Massachusetts or Connecticut, for example) would help enforce a strict religious conformity within its jurisdiction. And like the Anglicans, the Puritans would do their best to keep any other religious options closed. They, too, wanted to reproduce in America the European pattern of a church-state alliance.

During the 1630s, the Puritans rapidly grew stronger because of a large influx of immigrants from England. Yet even in those early years, they found much difficulty in maintaining a perfect religious harmony. In 1635 one of their number, Roger Williams, argued strongly that the church-state alliance pattern was totally wrong: one need only look at Europe's bloody religious wars to see that this is not what a God of love and mercy would want. Nothing was more absurd, Williams contended, than "the setting up of civil power and officers to judge the conviction of men's souls." He pointed out that the European pattern had been followed for 1,400 years, since the days of the Roman Emperor Constantine, and had brought to all humankind not peace but a sword. So it was time

The General Court of Massachusetts banished Roger Williams in 1635 because he challenged the Puritans' control of the government. The following year he founded Rhode Island.

to abandon that discredited model and begin anew. The leaders of Massachusetts strongly disagreed. They banished Williams, who made his way on foot through January snows to create the new colony of Rhode Island, where liberty of conscience would be assured to every citizen.

A year after the founding of Rhode Island, Massachusetts contended against another rebellious citizen—this time a woman, Anne Hutchinson. Mother and midwife, Hutchinson also aspired to be a theologian, an occupation regarded as inappropriate for women. Moreover, Hutchinson's theology was not acceptable, for it seemed to break the close bond between religion and morality. Hutchinson argued that because salvation was a free gift of God, it was not a reward for a pure life, nor did it necessarily result in a more moral life. In maintaining her position, this dissenter rejected the authority of both the church and the state; she even suggested that she had revelations beyond those found in the Bible. Governor John Winthrop, seeing in this case as much of a threat to the political stability and church harmony of Massachusetts as Roger Williams had posed, decreed that Hutchinson too must be exiled:

> Forasmuch as you, Mrs. Hutchinson, have highly transgressed and offended, and forasmuch as you have [in] so many ways troubled the Church with your errors, . . . I do not only pronounce you worthy to be cast out, but I do cast you out, and in the name of Christ I do deliver you up to Satan that you may learn no more to blaspheme, to seduce, and to lie.

After a time in Rhode Island, Anne Hutchinson and her family migrated farther south to Long Island; there, in 1643, the Hutchinsons (except for one small daughter) were killed by Indians. In their continuing effort to maintain a religious monopoly in the 17th century, the authorities of the Massachusetts Bay Colony repeatedly had to resort to imprisonment, fines, expulsions, or worse. The sect known as Quakers, despised in Winthrop's Massachusetts as in Cornbury's New York, proclaimed their message with courage and persistence. Their teaching that

John Winthrop, governor of the Massachusetts colony for 12 years, believed that the Bay Colony required a close alliance between the political and religious leaders. The Colony also required a faithful submission to God, for—in Winthrop's words—"we are entered into covenant with Him for this work."

The Quakers and Mary Dyer

The Quakers, more formally known as the Society of Friends, arose in England in 1651. In the first decade or so of their existence as a new sect, the followers of founder George Fox were zealously, even fanatically, evangelistic. Quaker missionaries spread quickly, not only over all of Britain and Ireland, but to North America as well. They would not be discouraged or silenced—as is obvious from the tragic case of Mary Dyer.

Mary Dyer was part of the large Puritan migration to New England in the 1630s. When Anne Hutchinson was expelled from Massachusetts because of her unorthodox religious views, a sympathetic Mary Dyer, along with her husband, William, accompanied Hutchinson to Rhode Island. In 1652, the Dyers returned briefly to England, where Mary joined the new Quaker movement. With all of the enthusiasm of a fresh convert, Mary Dyer returned to New England to spread the word of this upstart sect. In Massachusetts she was jailed, then expelled, then warned that she would be put to death if she returned to Boston. She did return in May 1660, and on June 1 she was hanged. This is part of her address to the Massachusetts General Court.

Whereas I am by many charged with the guiltiness of my own blood—if you mean in my coming to Boston—I am therein clear and justified by the Lord, in whose will I came. [He] will require my blood of you, be sure, who have made a law to take away the lives of the innocent servants of God if they come among you. [They] are called by you, "Cursed Quakers," although I say, and am a living witness for them and the Lord, that He hath blessed them, and sent them unto you.

Therefore, be not found fighters against God, but let my counsel and request be accepted with you: to repeal all such laws that the truth and servants of the Lord may have free passage among you, and be kept from shedding of innocent blood. . . . Nor can the enemy that stirreth you up thus to destroy this Holy Seed in any measure countervail the great damage that you will, by thus doing, procure. Therefore, seeing the Lord hath not hid it from me, it lieth upon me, in love to your souls, thus to persuade you. I have no [selfish] ends, the Lord knoweth, for if my life were freely granted by you, it would not avail me . . . so long as I should daily hear or see the sufferings of these people, my dear brethren and Seed, with whom my life is bound up. . . .

Was ever the like laws heard of, among a people that profess Christ come in the flesh? And you have . . . no other weapons but such laws to fight against "Spiritual Wickedness," as you call it? Woe is me for you! Of whom take you counsel? Search with the light of Christ in ye, and it will show you . . . who have been disobedient and deceived, as now you are. [The Inner] Light, as you come into [it], and obeying what is made manifest to you therein, [will convince you to] repent that you were [not] kept from shedding blood, though it were from a woman.

This statue of Mary Dyer was erected at the State House in Boston in 1959, almost 300 years after her hanging on the Common.

The Toleration Act passed by the Maryland Assembly in 1649 is considered a milestone of religious freedom. The act foreshadowed the Bill of Rights, though its freedoms were limited to Christians.

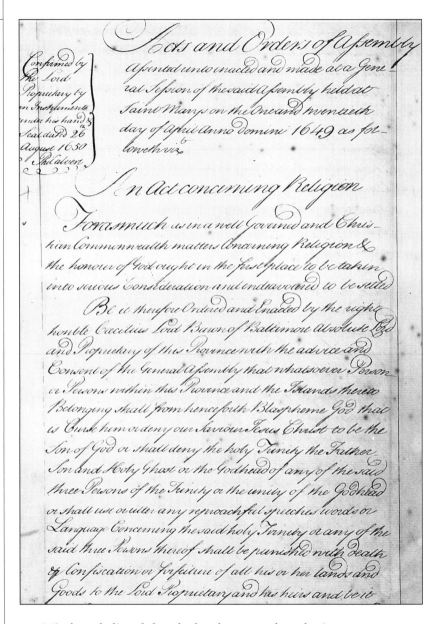

Winthrop believed that the burden upon the colonists was as great as their opportunity to be faithful and obedient Christians. "We shall be as a city on a hill," he told his followers, "the eyes of all people are upon us." As a reward for faith, God "shall make us a praise and glory." But, Winthrop concluded, if the colonists abandoned their faith, if they turned toward evil and sought only their own private welfare, then God would withdraw his protection and support: "We shall open the mouths of enemies to speak evil of the ways of God . . . we shall shame the faces of many of God's worthy servants, and cause their prayers to be turned into curses upon us till we be consumed out of the good land whither we are going."

This was the grand and noble vision that sustained the Puritans through physical hardship, meager food supplies, criticism from abroad, and dissent at home. But events continued to conspire against this New England effort to reproduce a Europe in America. During the 1690s a wave of hysteria resulted in tragedy. Many innocent people were hanged after being convicted of serving as instruments of Satan. Belief in satanic activity, witches, and wizards was widespread in the 17th century, and punishment by death was likewise common, even more so in Europe than in America. None of this, however, removed the stain from New England's leadership for allowing this fever to run unchecked until twenty people in Salem Village alone were put to death in 1692.

Some of the victims even acknowledged their guilt: that is, they believed that they were being used by Satan, or that they were "demon-possessed." Others, however, protested their innocence, arguing that they had made no pact with the devil and were being falsely accused. Rebecca Nurse, a pious wife and mother charged with witchcraft in June 1692, found to her amazement that friends and neighbors—though not her own family—were prepared to offer testimony against her. As wild rumors circulated about her, the bewildered Nurse wondered aloud "what sin hath God found out in me unrepented of, that He should lay such an affliction upon me in my old age?" On July 19, Rebecca Nurse, along with four other women, was hanged on what came to be called Gallows Hill.

Eventually, the hysteria passed. Some of the accusers begged to be forgiven, one of the judges confessed his error before his church, and a repentant clergyman admitted that "we walked in clouds and could not see our way." But damage to the establishment was done, as communities were divided and friendships destroyed.

The churches suffered even more directly during the years of religious revivalism, often called the Great Awakening, in the 18th century.

Revivals of religious feeling typically involved passionate preaching, followed by anxious concern of the hearers about the state of their souls and the conviction that they needed to confess their sins and turn away from wickedness. In 1741–42, tensions between pro-revivalists and anti-revivalists reached their height. "That was a time," one critic wrote, "when the superstitious panic ran very high, and bore down everybody that was not well fixed and established either by a natural steadiness of temper, or by strong reason and reflection."

Those who favored the revival regarded it as a genuine work of God, leading to the conversion of many and the moral reformation of many more. One Boston pastor reported with jubilation: "God is pleased to pour out His Spirit upon His people, and then His works of grace are as the light which goeth forth. . . . Convictions and conversions become more frequent and apparent. . . . Persons that were before quietly in their sins and unconcerned are so awakened that they can't stifle their convictions nor conceal their distress."

On the other hand, those who opposed the revival as overly emotional and bitterly divisive pointed to every extravagance in behavior or peculiarity in belief. The critics denounced traveling preachers as ignorant rabble-rousers, mere "peddlers in divinity." A pastor in Hartford, Connecticut, cried out: "Can nothing be done to heal our unhappy divisions?" He blamed the revivalist party for "unscriptural separations and disorderly practices of various kinds which have a direct tendency to . . . disturb the peace of this our Jerusalem and greatly weaken the wall of it."

And so New England, which had long presented a united front in religious matters, now found itself noisily and embarrassingly divided. Those divisions grew worse as Quakers and Baptists, then Methodists and even Anglicans aggravated the tensions or took advantage of the separations within the Congregational Church. On a popular level, many inhabitants turned from the approved orthodoxy to practice magic, compose astrological charts, and keep alive countless superstitions that seem never to die. Congregationalists continued to dominate the halls of power and the educational centers such as Harvard and Yale Colleges, but the iron bands of a religious monopoly had been broken. From the very beginning of colonial history, transplanting European patterns onto the American scene proved difficult. By the end of the colonial period, such a transfer had proved to be impossible.

Try as they might to impose uniformity, New Englanders could not ignore the presence of Rhode Island, with its steely determination to keep church and state apart. Farther south, the colony of Maryland had been created as a refuge for England's still-persecuted Roman Catholics. Yet Maryland's founder, Lord Baltimore, never intended the colony to be for Catholics only. And to make that intention explicit, the Maryland Assembly in 1649 passed a Toleration Act that guaranteed to all Christians the right of worship in accordance with their own consciences.

In 1664 the Proprietors of New Jersey echoed the language of Rhode Island's liberal charter of the previous year, assuring all potential settlers that they would not in any way be "molested, punished, disquieted or called into question" for any difference in religious opinion or practice. Carolina followed suit in 1665, and in 1682 Pennsylvania was even more emphatic, under the guidance of the English Quaker William Penn. Slowly but steadily, an American pattern of religious liberty displaced the European pattern of a single national church.

In the last quarter of the 18th century, the American Revolution made these tentative moves by individual colonies more nearly a model to be followed by all. The revolution dedicated itself, quite openly, to the achievement of liberty, both civil and ecclesiastical. In the eyes of many colonists, political liberty was meaningless unless it guaranteed that most precious of all liberties—the freedom of the soul. And religious liberty was never secure so long as political tyrants sat upon the throne. Or, as James Madison put it, "Torrents of blood have been spilt in the old world, by vain attempts of the secular arm to extinguish religious discord. . . . Time has at length revealed the true remedy." That remedy was a full and free religious liberty in a new and independent nation. This was and is the essence of "the American experiment."

Chapter 2

A New Nation: The American Experiment

Two centuries or more after the American Revolution, it is difficult to believe that this war of independence was fought for religious liberty no less than political liberty. The colonists declared that they were resisting the political tyranny of Great Britain, but any victory in that regard would have been hollow if Americans could not enjoy full liberty of conscience. Historically, Britain had imposed its political will side by side with its spiritual will upon all its subjects, at home and abroad. In the 1760s and 1770s, many Americans were determined that this would never be the case should they achieve independence.

An early indication of American determination was the firm refusal to allow Church of England bishops to reside in the colonies. At first glance, this may seem an unlikely place to draw a line in the sand. Were not bishops kindly souls who watched over their flocks and cared for their spiritual needs? Who could be anxious about such respected gentlemen sailing across the ocean to settle in Virginia or New York?

In 17th-century England, bishops wielded enormous political as well as spiritual power. Bishops were officers of the state, members of the powerful House of Lords, agents of persecution and oppression. And much of this bad odor clung to bishops in the 18th century as well. Many Americans had fled England just to escape the authority of these all-powerful figures. The very thought of religious officials wielding similar

Thomas Bradbury Chandler, a New Jersey minister, demanded a greater freedom for the Anglican Church in America. He argued that "unless Bishops should be speedily sent us, we can foresee nothing but the ruin of the Church in this country."

powers in America inflamed the colonists' passions to great heights and contributed to their readiness to sever their ties with England.

This deep anxiety was evident in 1767, when an Anglican clergyman in New Jersey, Thomas Bradbury Chandler, published *An Appeal to the Public,* arguing that bishops should reside in America. He asserted that bishops were necessary for the complete operation of the Church of England, for only bishops could confer full membership upon potential converts and ordain young men into the Anglican ministry. To deny us our bishops, Chandler affirmed, is to deny us our religious liberty. He rebutted opponents who worried about being taxed (as in England) for the support of bishops and their "palaces." Americans would not be taxed, he said, and if they were, the tax would be a small one: 4 pennies per 100 pounds sterling. "And this would be no mighty hardship upon the country," Chandler asserted. In fact, anyone that objected to giving 1/6000th of his income to any cause should not be considered "a good subject." Then, misjudging the mood of Americans even more, Chandler argued that bishops were necessary to support the monarchy. "Episcopacy [that is, rule by bishops] can never thrive in a republican government, nor republican principles in an Episcopal Church." Such an argument, made two years after widespread American objections to the Stamp Act, which levied taxes on Americans without their consent, was unlikely to find broad support.

Chandler had thrown down the gauntlet, and a Presbyterian lawyer, William Livingston, quickly picked it up. He attacked Chandler and all in America or England who supported him. In 1768 Livingston even launched a newspaper "war" with letters to the *New York Gazette* and the *Weekly Mercury.* Chandler had adopted a moderate tone, Livingston noted, thereby possibly deluding many who do not detect the wolf hiding in sheep's clothing. Under these circumstances, "I cannot but think it my duty to administer an antidote to the poison" and to point out all errors of fact as well as of reasoning. Livingston went through Chandler's arguments one by one in order to demonstrate that the Anglican clergymen would "introduce an evil more terrible to every man who sets a proper value either on his liberty, property, or conscience than the so greatly and deservedly obnoxious Stamp Act itself."

For Americans in the last third of the 18th century, any threat to religious liberty was a threat to *all* liberty. Ezra Stiles, president of Yale College, noted in 1769 that the effort to introduce Anglican bishops to America would result in "our civil liberties" being placed "in eminent danger." He added: "We have so long tasted [the] sweets of civil and religious liberty that we cannot be easily prevailed upon to submit to a yoke of bondage which neither we nor our Fathers were able to bear." The more that Anglicans campaigned for their cause, the more the opposition grew.

William Livingston, a lawyer, understood that religious and political freedom were inseparable. In condemning the power of the Anglican Church he was also condemning the power of England. Both cramped America's freedom.

As John Adams later observed regarding the causes of the American Revolution, the 1760s saw "a universal alarm against the authority of Parliament" rapidly rising. The Chandler *Appeal* and others like it "excited a general and just apprehension that bishops and dioceses and churches and priests and tithes [ecclesiastical taxes] were to be imposed by Parliament," Adams noted. And he concluded that "if Parliament could tax us, they could establish the Church of England with all its creeds, articles, tests, ceremonies, and tithes." The amount of the tax was never the issue; the principle involved in accepting such a tax surely was.

The strength of the opposition to Anglican bishops can be measured in many ways, among them the striking fact that no such bishop ever arrived in colonial America. The opposing forces included, of course, Baptists, Quakers, Lutherans, Dutch Reformed, Presbyterians, Congregationalists, Roman Catholics, and even a good many Anglicans, particularly in the southern colonies. In 1771, Richard Bland, a member of the Virginia General Assembly and a loyal Anglican, declared that bringing bishops to America "will produce greater convulsions than anything that has as yet happened in this part of the globe." He wisely added that "a religious dispute is the most fierce and destructive of all others to the peace and happiness of government." America would not import England's intolerance or Europe's religious wars.

As the revolutionary fervor mounted in the 1770s, Anglican missionaries sent out by London's Society for the Propagation of the Gospel aroused resentment for their loyalty to England and for their resistance to the cause of independence. One such missionary, Thomas Barton, assigned to a parish in Lancaster, Pennsylvania, found life intolerable after the Declaration of Independence was adopted in July 1776. In November of that year, he reported to his superiors in England, "I have been obliged to shut my churches to avoid the fury of the populace who would not [allow] the liturgy to be used unless the . . . prayers for the King and Royal Family were omitted." Barton reported that other Anglican missionaries "have been dragged from their horses, assaulted with stones and dirt, ducked in water, obliged to flee for their lives, driven from their habitations and families, laid under arrest and imprisoned!" The American Revolution was a time of high passion, and a good deal of that passion was religious in motivation and expression.

In 1776, of course, it was far from clear who would win the war for independence. Many Tories, loyal to England for political, economic, and religious reasons, thought it only a matter of months before England reasserted control. A New York Anglican, Charles Inglis, characterized the patriot uprising as "one of the most causeless, unprovoked, and unnatural that ever disgraced any country." He was confident that it would soon blow over. After all, England was the major world power, recently victorious over France in the

The Anglican missionary shown on this bookplate brings the word of God to the New World. Despite the work of such organizations as the Society for Propagating the Gospel, the Church of England failed to maintain a religious monopoly anywhere in colonial America.

Seven Years War. With a powerful navy and an experienced army, England had grown accustomed to rule in civil as well as religious affairs. The United States, on the other hand, had no standing army, no seaworthy navy, no national treasury on which to draw, and no political unity that could be depended on. All they had in 1776 was a passionate commitment to liberty, both civil and religious.

By 1783, when the United States gained its official independence through the Treaty of Paris, the tables had turned. A victorious nation would not soon forget the suffering and deprivation of the long war. Nor would it forget the clear purposes of that war. Indeed, as early as 1776 Virginians and others moved to disestablish the Church of England in their respective states: that is, to cut all ties between the church and the state, to stop enforcing any sort of religious conformity in either belief or behavior, and above all to stop collecting taxes from all for the religious benefit of a few.

But disestablishment was essentially a negative action. Thomas Jefferson, along with others, wanted to take a more positive step: namely, to guarantee religious liberty to all Virginia's citizens. As early as 1777,

This dramatic engraving of the burning of Washington in 1814 attests to England's powerful and experienced army. Although the British took all major American cities, they were eventually defeated by the Revolutionaries.

Jefferson composed a Bill for Establishing Religious Freedom. When Jefferson became governor in 1779, he promptly introduced his bill to the legislators, only to see them quickly table the measure for an indefinite period. Many legislators thought that Virginia was not yet ready to take so radical and abrupt a step. After all, the revolution had not yet been won; the state had not yet secured its firm social and cultural foundation. In 1781, when the cannons were stilled, Jefferson continued to believe that no liberty was secure unless liberty in religion was explicitly guaranteed. When he accepted an appointment as the U.S. minister to France in 1785, he could no longer follow the fortunes of his proposed law as closely as before. Now he had to depend on the wisdom and skill of a younger colleague and neighbor, James Madison.

Madison needed no encouragement to take up the cause of religious liberty. In 1774, when only 22 years of age, Madison had written to a classmate at the College of New Jersey (now Princeton University) to express his displeasure over the Anglican effort in Virginia to drive out or suppress all other churches but its own. When state authorities threw some Baptist traveling preachers in jail for merely declaring their own religious opinions, they resorted once again, said Madison, to that "diabolical, hell-conceived principle of persecution." Even before the revolution, Madison saw religious freedom as the only proper path for all Americans to take. In Virginia, he wrote, "Religious bondage shackles and debilitates the mind and unfits it for every noble enterprise, every expanded prospect." True religion, he concluded, could be propagated only by reason and persuasion, never by power and the sword.

Once the Treaty of Paris was signed, the Virginia legislature could safely turn its attention again to domestic matters, including the appropriate legal status for religion. Returning from three years of service in the Continental Congress in Philadelphia, Madison was elected to Virginia's legislative assembly in 1784. There, with or without Jefferson, he stood ready to enlist as many citizens as possible in the sacred cause of religious freedom.

At this juncture, some Virginians looked for a middle path between the disestablishment of the Anglican Church on the one hand and the

Patrick Henry won his oratorical fame in the "Give Me Liberty or Give Me Death" speech, delivered in St. John's Episcopal Church in Richmond, Virginia, March 23, 1775.

assertion of a complete religious liberty on the other. But did any such middle path exist? Patrick Henry, the famous Virginia orator, joined with some others in proposing what seemed a happy compromise. The Church of England should not continue to enjoy special favor and privilege—that was agreed. But how about a special status for Christianity itself? Could not most Virginians see some advantage extending governmental favor to all their churches? After all, Virginia had for nearly 200 years supported an alliance between the civil and the ecclesiastical realms. Should all this be abruptly, even brutally, abolished? Many thought a more gradual approach the wiser course of action.

Thomas Jefferson's Statute for Establishing Religious Freedom (passed by Virginia's General Assembly, January 16, 1786)

Whereas Almighty God hath created the mind free; that all attempts to influence it by temporal punishments or burthens, or by civil incapacitations, tend only to beget habits of hypocrisy and meanness, and are a departure from the plan of the Holy author of our religion, who being Lord both of body and mind, yet chose not to propagate it by coercions on either, as was in his Almighty power to do; . . .

[and whereas] the impious presumption of legislators and rulers, civil as well as ecclesiastical, who being themselves but fallible and uninspired men, have assumed dominion over the faith of others, setting up their own opinions and modes of thinking as the only true and infallible, and as such endeavoring to impose them upon others, hath established and maintained false religions over the greatest part of the world, and through all time; . . .

[and whereas] our civil rights have no dependence on our religious opinions, any more than our opinions in physics or geometry; . . .

and finally, [whereas] truth is great and will prevail if left to herself, that she is the proper and sufficient antagonist to error, and has nothing to fear from the conflict, unless by human interposition disarmed of her natural weapons, free argument and debate, errors ceasing to be dangerous when it is permitted freely to contradict them:

Be it enacted by the General Assembly, That no man shall be compelled to frequent or support any religious worship, place, or ministry whatsoever, nor shall be enforced, restrained, molested, or burthened in his body or goods, nor shall otherwise suffer on account of his religious opinions or belief; but that all men shall be free to profess, and by argument to maintain, their opinion in matters of religion, and that the same shall in no wise diminish, enlarge, or affect their civil capacities.

have produced the first legislature who has had the courage to declare that the reason of man may be trusted with the formation of his own opinions." He requested that on his tombstone, he be remembered for the writing of only two documents: the Declaration of Independence and the Statute for Establishing Religious Freedom.

A year and a half after the passage of Jefferson's statute, delegates met in Philadelphia to draw up a new frame of government for the whole nation. George Washington, the most trusted person in the country, presided over this Constitutional Convention, while the aged patriarch of 81 years, Benjamin Franklin, lent his wit and gentle wisdom to the assembly. As the delegates struggled to find some consensus, Franklin urged that prayers be offered as they had been during the revolution. "I have lived, Sir, a long time," said Franklin in addressing the chair, "and the longer I live, the more convincing proofs I see of this truth—that God governs in the affairs of men." Then Franklin added that if a sparrow cannot fall to the ground without God's notice, "is it probable that an empire can rise without his aid?" But Franklin persuaded few of his fellows to introduce prayer into their deliberations. A wild rumor even circulated that Alexander Hamilton had said that the delegates should not at this point call upon foreign aid. What he really said, however, was that to introduce prayer at that point, rather than at the beginning of the convention, might lead the public to believe that the delegates had reached some serious disagreement or impasse.

The most acute mind at the convention belonged to James Madison, who saw the delegates' task as that of writing a secular document for a civil state. Religion did not figure prominently in the discussion and debate. In fact, in the Constitution itself religion receives only a single mention (in Article 6) and that a negative one: "No religious Test shall ever be required as a Qualification to any office or public Trust under the United States." In the realm of religion, the silences of the Constitution were more surprising than its explicit phrases. Unlike most state constitutions of the time, the national document did not mention God even in the vaguest terms of an "overruling Providence" or "Grand Architect" of the world or acknowledge the existence of any national creed. To many these silences were offensive, for they seemed to sever all ties between the federal government and Christianity, or between the nation and any religion at all. And when the Constitution did speak, it opened the door for persons of any faith, or no faith at all, to serve as President of the United States.

In the state conventions called to ratify or reject the newly drafted U.S. Constitution, the "no religious test" phrase obviously rankled many delegates. In New Hampshire, one delegate rejected the Constitution because under its terms "we may have a Papist, a Mohomatan, a Deist, yea an Atheist at the helm of Government." In Massachusetts, opponents argued that all nations acknowledged the need of religion, which had "a direct tendency to secure the practice of good morals and consequently the peace of society." And in Pennsylvania one writer thought that the Constitution, by eliminating ties to religion, paved the way for the central government to become arbitrary and absolute, since it recognized no higher law than itself.

Others, however, remembered how religious tests had been used in England to exclude from public office not only Roman Catholics but all Protestant dissenters as well. Religious tests in Italy, Portugal, Spain, and elsewhere had functioned as engines of persecution, a Connecticut delegate observed, and as invitations to hypocrisy and deceit. The only people excluded by religious tests were the honest and the conscientious. In England, "the most abandoned characters partake of the [Anglican] sacrament, in order to qualify themselves for public employment."

Even more troubling to a great many was the failure of the Constitution to provide for a full religious liberty along with other fundamental freedoms. When Madison sent a copy of the proposed Constitution to Thomas Jefferson in Paris, the latter responded first with his compliments, then with his objections. "I will now add what I do not like. First, the omission of a bill of rights providing clearly and without the aid of sophisms for the freedom of religion" and other liberties appropriate to a republic. Jefferson listed religious freedom first, for in his mind it was and would always be the foundation on which all other freedoms rested. By the time that Madison received Jefferson's reply, he had already learned that many citizens would refuse to ratify a Constitution without a Bill of Rights, or at least an explicit assurance that such a bill would be the first order of business in the newly established Congress. As one of those elected to the House of Representatives, Madison gave his word, especially to his fellow Virginians, that he would immediately press for explicit guarantees of fundamental freedoms. Even so, the vote for ratification in Virginia was a close one (89 in favor, 79 opposed), as it was in several other critical states.

When the Constitution was finally ratified by a sufficient number of states (9 out of 13) and George Washington assumed the office of President, many religious minorities were clearly nervous about what a stronger central government might mean to their freedom. Jews in Newport, Rhode Island, for example, seized the opportunity of Washington's visit to Newport in 1790 to praise a new government "which gives no sanction to bigotry and no assistance to persecution, but generously afford[s] to all liberties of conscience and immunities of citizenship." When Washington returned to New York (the national capital at that time), he wrote to the Newport congregation, expressing his assurances concerning liberty of conscience. He also noted that the United States had moved beyond an age of mere "toleration" to a full recognition of the natural rights of all humankind. "The Government of the United States," he concluded,

Independence Hall in Philadelphia housed the Constitutional Convention of 1787. Political concerns dominated the meeting, and religion received only one mention in the Constitution.

The Bill of Rights was ratified in 1791 to ensure that
fundamental liberties such
as freedom of religion
would not be violated by
the federal government.

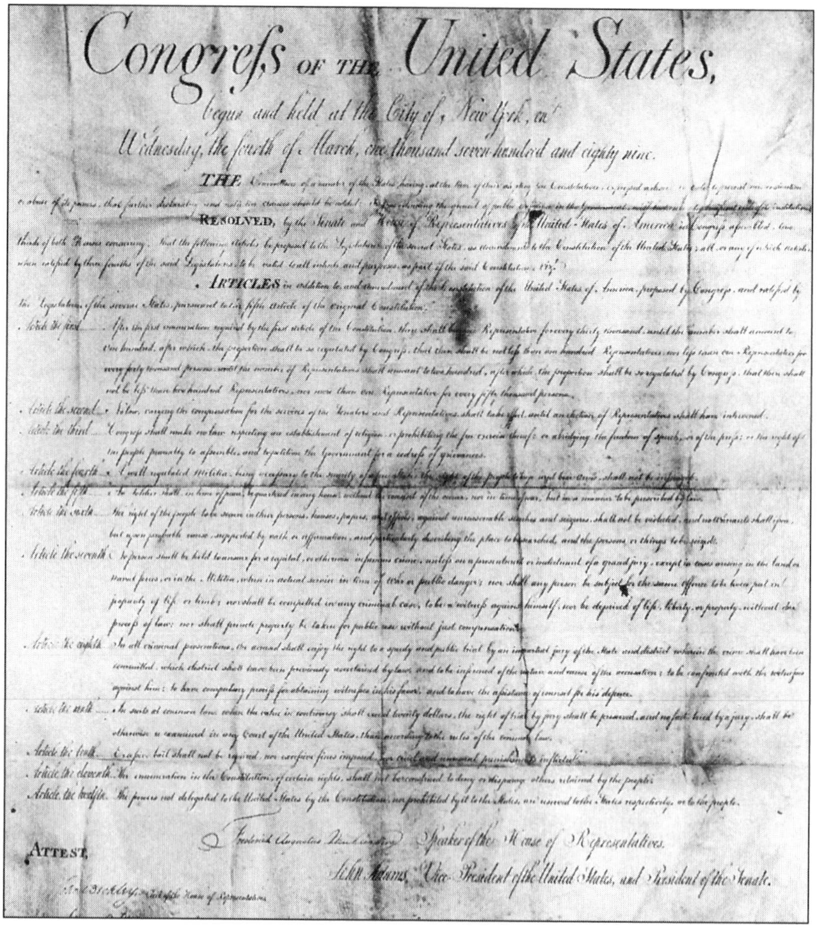

"which gives to bigotry no sanction, to persecution no assistance, requires only that they who live under its protection should demean themselves as good citizens in giving it on all occasions their effectual support." Roman Catholics, Baptists, Quakers, and others received similar reassurances from the President concerning their religious freedoms. But something more than private guarantees was required.

In June 1789 Madison introduced a Bill of Rights, as he had promised his fellow Virginians that he would do. The phrases of the First Amendment that dealt with religion went through many modifications and changes between June and September, when the final wording was agreed upon. On June 7 Madison proposed this language: "The Civil

Rights of none shall be abridged on account of religious belief or worship, nor shall any national religion be established, nor shall the full and equal rights of conscience be in any manner, nor on any pretext infringed." By the end of July the House Select Committee had abridged Madison's 40 words down to 16: "No religion shall be established by law, nor shall the equal rights of conscience be infringed." After another month of debate, the House's wording was sent to the Senate for reflection and refinement. At the end of September both House and Senate agreed on a final version. And so the First Amendment, as ratified by the states in 1791, begins with these words: "Congress shall make no law respecting an establishment of religion, or prohibiting the free exercise thereof."

Because these crucial words would occupy the Supreme Court and other courts for the next 200 years and beyond, it is important to understand their meaning. The first of the two clauses, "Congress shall make no law respecting an establishment of religion," is for obvious reasons regularly referred to, in a kind of legal shorthand, as "the establishment clause." It prohibits Congress from favoring or advancing religion, certainly from elevating any one religion above another. The second clause, "the free exercise clause," places another kind of limit on the national government: it may do nothing to interfere with or suppress one's religious devotion or belief. Religious freedom has, therefore, a double guarantee—the only constitutional liberty of which this is true. Congress can render no aid; Congress can do no harm.

Of course, the meaning of the First Amendment is far from simple in actual practice. The courts, the churches, and the citizenry at large have wrestled with both of these clauses, again and again, rarely arriving—at least in recent decades—at an interpretation that is unanimous or beyond all controversy.

The 19th Century: A Quiet Court

Religion without governmental sanction or support: How would this actually work out in a rapidly expanding nation? No one was quite sure. Those denominations long accustomed to official help, for example, the Congregationalists in New England and the Episcopalians elsewhere, ventured onto the boisterous seas of religious liberty with some caution and fear. Other denominations, such as the Baptists and the newly organized Methodists, found the rough waters bracing and challenging. And those religious bodies that saw liberty chiefly in terms of the opportunities that it presented flourished dramatically. By 1850, for example, Methodists and Baptists together had roughly seven times the number of churches as Congregationalists and Episcopalians together. The profile of American religion was rapidly changing.

The key word to describe this "new look" among the churches was voluntarism. A whole host of voluntary societies arose early in the 19th century to meet needs that government would not or could not serve: the American Bible Society (founded 1816), which made inexpensive copies of the Bible widely available on the frontier and elsewhere; the American Sunday School Union (1824), which encouraged the establishment of Sunday schools, often led by women, even where no churches were found; the American Tract Society (1825), which printed moral and

During the 19th century, religious activity came to depend on volunteers, such as this Civil War chaplain preaching to a crowd of soldiers at Camp Dick Robinson, Kentucky, in 1861.

This daguerreotype of the preacher Lyman Beecher captures his steel will. He held Congregational or Presbyterian pastorates in East Hampton, New York; Litchfield, Connecticut; Boston; and Cincinnati, Ohio.

For two decades or more, the legislature wrestled with this issue and with the rising public resentment. Then in 1802 it ordered that these glebe lands be sold for the benefit of all the citizens of the state. The Episcopal Church understandably protested and decided that justice would more likely come through the courts than through the legislature. The Supreme Court finally heard the case (*Terret* v. *Taylor*) in 1815 and determined—not on First Amendment grounds, but by the "maxims of eternal justice"—that the American Revolution had not destroyed the civil rights of corporations any more than of individuals. Insofar as possible, said the Court, glebe lands should be returned to the Episcopal Church or to the private owners who held title to the property before 1776.

For those who thought that the U. S. Constitution should make a clean break between old patterns and new, this decision was a defeat. But in other more serious instances of cultural or legal lag, victory awaited. In New England (except for Rhode Island), Congregationalism continued to be the established church well into the 19th century. An obvious question arises: How could this be after a First Amendment had been adopted in 1791? But it must be recalled that the amendment stated, "*Congress* shall make no law. . . ." It said nothing about what the states might or might not do with respect to the establishment of religion. And so in Connecticut, for example, the Congregational Church was still supported by taxes and still enjoyed special privileges on election days, militia training days, and other state occasions. Members of other denominations, especially the Baptists, Quakers, and Episcopalians, naturally protested this long delay in catching up with the "Spirit of '76." But for decades their protests fell on deaf ears.

Finally in 1818, in a close state referendum, the Jeffersonian party prevailed over the Federalists, and the last ties of the church to the state were severed. Jefferson wrote to John Adams of his pleasure that "this den of priesthood is at length broken up and that a Protestant popedom is no longer to disgrace the American history and character." One might expect

such a sentiment from Thomas Jefferson, but even some Congregationalists later agreed that disestablishment turned out to be healthy both
for the church and the state. Lyman Beecher, the Congregational pastor in
Litchfield, worked as hard as he could on the Federalist side to preserve
the church-state connection. In his autobiography, he recalled that he
lobbied and preached "with all my might" to defeat the dissenters and the
Jeffersonians and called his defeat "as dark a day as ever I saw." Yet this
setback, Beecher confessed, proved to be "the best thing that ever happened to the state of Connecticut." For, he explained, "It cut the churches
loose from dependence on state support. It threw them wholly on their
own resources and on God."

The year after disestablishment in Connecticut, the U.S. Supreme
Court rendered an important decision that preserved and protected the
role of the churches in the founding of denominational colleges. The case
(*Dartmouth College* v. *Woodward,* 1819) concerned Dartmouth College,
which had been founded under Congregational auspices in New

In 1819 the U.S. Supreme
Court ruled that
Dartmouth College could
remain a Congregational
institution. This served to
protect other religious colleges from hostile government takeovers.

In his long tenure as Chief Justice of the United States (1801-1835), John Marshall did much to bring the judicial branch of the federal government to a level equal with the executive and legislative branches.

Hampshire in 1769. Because the state of New Hampshire had no other institution of higher education, some thought that after the revolution it made perfect sense to transform Dartmouth into a public university. Dartmouth should belong to all the citizens of the state, so the argument went, and not just to the members of a single sect. The governor of the state, William Plumer, even convinced the legislature to assert its control over the school.

At this point, a skilled lawyer and orator who also happened to be an alumnus of Dartmouth stepped into the picture. Daniel Webster took the college's case to the Supreme Court, where he effectively argued that the colonial charter had not been voided by the War of Independence. The 12 Congregational trustees and their successors still retained their sole right of ownership and operation of the school, free from any "forcible intrusion of others." According to an unofficial report, Webster concluded his argument with these passionate words: "It is, Sir, as I have said, a small College. And yet there are those who love it." He said that when he observed his school being stabbed again and again, like Caesar in the Roman Senate, he could not bear the thought of his alma mater turning to him in sorrow and dismay, saying "And thou too, my son!"

Chief Justice John Marshall, convinced that Webster was right, ruled that the original contract or charter could not be voided or violated in this manner. Any such attempt, he added, would be "repugnant to the Constitution of the United States." And so the private and religious character of Dartmouth was saved. Even more important, the scores of denominational colleges already in existence or then being contemplated now had legal protection against hostile takeovers. If the state of New Hampshire or any other state wanted its own public university, it would have to be created afresh, not appropriated from any denomination or church.

Meanwhile, the state of Massachusetts continued to cling to its official Congregationalism. There, the picture was muddied by internal ecclesiastical struggles between orthodox Congregationalists (who believed in the Trinity: God the Father, God the Son, and God the Spirit) and the rise of Unitarians (who believed in the unity or oneness of God). The U.S. Supreme Court did not get involved in the many quarrels over property, taxation, election of ministers, and the like, but the Massachusetts Supreme Court did. In an important case heard in 1820 (*Baker* v. *Fales*), the liberal Unitarians won their claim to the original church property. Indirectly, the case demonstrated the glaring absurdity of trying to maintain an established church so long after religious freedom prevailed everywhere else in the country. In 1831 the Massachusetts legislature voted for disestablishment, but since this required an amendment to the state constitution, the matter had to be submitted to a vote of the people. In 1833 the citizens of Massachusetts, by a margin of almost 10 to 1, voted to bring the longstanding church-state alliance to an end. Of the original Founding Fathers, only James Madison lived long enough to see the curtain fall on this last vestige of an era now gone by.

Throughout the country, other religious controversies in the first half of the 19th century often ended up in the lower courts, since usually only state or local laws were involved. These disputes concerned such matters as Sunday mails, the ownership of church property, the purity of church doctrine, the nature of church government, and even appropriate punishments for blasphemy. Regarding the first of these issues, Congress in 1810 passed a law requiring post offices to stay open every day "on which a mail or bag, or other packet or parcel of letters shall arrive." The law aroused much opposition among those who regarded Sunday as a day set aside strictly for rest and worship. Moreover, a few states that had laws prohibiting travel on Sundays thought that this prohibition should apply to the federal mails as well.

During the administration of President Andrew Jackson, a major campaign was undertaken to ban the movement of mail on Sundays and to require all post offices to be closed on that day. Senator Richard M. Johnson of Kentucky, who chaired the Senate committee having oversight of the post office, resisted this campaign in the name of religious

Public recreational events in the 19th century, such as the 1893 Columbian Exposition in Chicago, were allowed to be open on Sundays. Over the years the U.S. Supreme Court handed down many rulings concerning the Sunday laws passed by cities or states.

neutrality and church-state separation. "The transportation of the mail on the first day of the week," Johnson said, "does not interfere with the rights of conscience." Those who argue otherwise, he added, do so on the basis of a particular religious position and on the grounds that the present practice is "a violation of the law of God." Should Congress adopt their position, "it would establish the principle that the Legislature is a proper tribunal to determine what are the laws of God." And that, Johnson concluded, could not be, for "the constitution has wisely withheld from our Government the power of defining divine law."

Senator Johnson and his committee prevailed; the mail continued to travel on Sunday, and most post offices continued to be open on that day, at least long enough to receive the mail. Below the federal level, however, a whole universe of Sunday law cases opened up, to be heard by municipal and state courts and decided in a wide variety of ways. These cases dealt with such matters as what businesses (if any) could remain open on Sundays, what products (including newspapers) could be produced or sold, and what recreational activities (if any) could be allowed. In the 20th century, many of these issues did finally reach the U.S. Supreme Court.

In the 1840s and 1850s, the most passionate controversy of all concerned slavery. This bitter issue divided families, churches, and entire denominations (Baptist, Methodist, and Presbyterian), and ultimately the country itself. The major implication of the Civil War and its aftermath for church-state matters is found in the Fourteenth Amendment to the Constitution, adopted in 1868. That amendment reads as follows:

> No State shall make or enforce any law which shall abridge the privileges or immunities of citizens of the United States; nor shall any State deprive any person of life, liberty, or property, without due process of law; nor deny to any person within its jurisdiction the equal protection of the law.

An artistic portrayal of an African American slave responding to Abraham Lincoln's Emancipation Proclamation, issued in 1863. The Fourteenth Amendment was drafted to protect the civil rights of freed slaves.

Though crafted primarily to protect the civil rights of the former slaves, this amendment ultimately had implications far beyond this one area. The First Amendment, it must be recalled, limited itself to what the U.S. Congress could or could not do. Now, the Fourteenth Amendment spoke of what states may or may not do. In later years, this language was to have great effect on religious freedoms and government-bestowed religious favors.

Attitudes toward slavery and race led to the passage of the Fourteenth Amendment; they also led to the first case of internal church controversy to reach the Supreme Court. The case of *Watson* v. *Jones,* decided in 1872,

In 1838, Governor L.W. Boggs proclaimed that all Mormons were to be expelled from the state of Missouri or face extermination. The generals of the army, gathering in the court martial tent, discuss the execution of the Mormon leaders.

stemmed from a dispute in the Walnut Street Presbyterian Church in Louisville, Kentucky. In 1866 the General Assembly of the northern branch of the Presbyterian church decreed that church membership could not be granted to people who voluntarily aided the South in the Civil War or who believed in slavery as a divine institution. Some members of the congregation agreed with this decree; others did not. The dispute ultimately involved larger governing bodies within the denomination, with each side claiming to be true to Presbyterian rules of governance and Presbyterian doctrines of faith. And with respect to the specific congregation, each side staked its claim to the ownership of the church property and to the control of the church's finances.

The Supreme Court was not eager to enter into what seemed to be, after all, a private church dispute. But other ways of settling the troubled matter grew dim when Kentucky's highest court rendered one decision and the church's own court, the General Assembly, rendered another. So the U.S. Supreme Court felt obliged to take up the issue. Once having agreed to hear the case, however, the Court made a heroic effort to distinguish between the kinds of church controversies that the civil courts should deal with and those they should not. Many churches, the Court pointed out, had a "congregational" form of government: that is, the con-

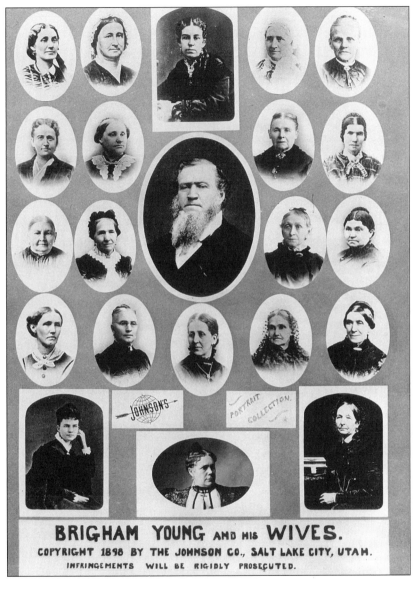

BRIGHAM YOUNG AND HIS WIVES.
COPYRIGHT 1898 BY THE JOHNSON CO., SALT LAKE CITY, UTAH.
INFRINGEMENTS WILL BE RIGIDLY PROSECUTED.

Brigham Young maintained the unity of the Mormon church after the assassination of Joseph Smith in 1844. The number of Young's wives is a matter of speculation to this day.

gregation had the final voice (as among Baptists, Congregationalists, Disciples of Christ, and others). In these instances, one need only count the votes of the church members. But many other churches had a "hierarchical" form of government: that is, higher authorities beyond the local church had the final voice (as among Presbyterians, Episcopalians, Roman Catholics, Eastern Orthodox, and others).

In these latter cases, the Court declared, "whenever the questions of discipline or of faith, or ecclesiastical rule, custom or law have been decided" by the highest authorities in the church, all federal courts "must accept such decisions as final." Other nations may act differently, Justice Samuel Miller admitted, but in the United States citizens have "the full and free right to entertain any religious belief, to practice any religious principle, and to teach any religious doctrine which does not violate the laws of morality and property" and does not infringe on personal rights. And this included the right to be governed by the denominations of which they were voluntarily a part. Federal courts should especially avoid trying to rule on church doctrine and belief. To emphasize its point, the Court pointed out that "the law knows no heresy, and is committed to the support of no dogma, the establishment of no sect." In *Watson* v. *Jones,* the Court ruled in favor of the denomination's General Assembly, even as it established a precedent for the Court to stay out of such cases in the future.

By far the most memorable judicial activities related to religion in the 19th century were what became known as "the Mormon cases." The practice of polygamy or "plural marriage" of one man to several wives, common among the Mormons of that time, gave rise to important decisions by the Supreme Court in 1879 and 1890. Long before its practices came before the Supreme Court, the Church of Jesus Christ of Latter-day Saints (to use the formal title of the institution created by Joseph Smith in 1830) had been an object of suspicion and hostility. First of all, Smith's church had added its own scripture, *The Book of Mormon,* to the Bible, which in the opinion of most other Christians did not need amending. Second, the Mormons scorned private property and practiced a type of communal living that set them apart from their neighbors. Third, and clearly most shocking of all, the Mormon faith sanctioned polygamy. In the first two decades of the church's life, the Mormons were driven from Ohio to Missouri to Illinois, where in 1844 Joseph Smith was assassinated. In 1847, the Mormons embarked on a final grand exodus out to the Salt Lake Basin in Utah, where they hoped to escape the animosities and persecutions that plagued them from the beginning.

But the creation of the Utah Territory by the federal government in 1850 meant that the United States would not forget the Mormons. In 1862 Congress outlawed polygamy in all U.S. territories. Twenty years later another federal law made it illegal for polygamists to vote or hold office. Party platforms called for an end to "that relic of barbarism, polygamy," and Congress even moved to confiscate the property of the Mormon Church. In this supercharged atmosphere, the Supreme Court heard *Reynolds* v. *United States* in 1879 and *Davis* v. *Beason* in 1890. These were church-state cases of major magnitude, and they aroused a fevered interest on the part of the public.

Under the 1862 law, George Reynolds, private secretary to Mormon leader Brigham Young, was indicted in 1875, convicted, and sentenced to two years of hard labor for the crime of bigamy: that is, being married to two women at the same time. He appealed his case all the way to the Supreme Court, which unanimously upheld the conviction of the lower court. Because this was the first case dealing explicitly with the free-exercise clause of the First Amendment, Chief Justice Morrison Waite thought it proper to review the history that led to the amendment. He included specific reference to Madison's *Memorial and Remonstrance* as well as to Jefferson's Bill for Establishing Religious Freedom in Virginia. He also set a significant precedent by citing Jefferson's "wall of separation" phrase from 1802.

But Waite then explained that although the First Amendment deprived Congress "of all legislative power over mere opinion," it "was left free to reach actions which were in violation of social duties or subversive of good order." Polygamy (or in this case, bigamy), in the Court's opinion, fell squarely in the category of such actions. "It is impossible to believe," Waite noted, "that the constitutional guaranty of religious freedom was intended to prohibit legislation [such as the law of 1862] in respect to this most important feature of social life." Then he raised a central question: "Can a man excuse his practices [contrary to law] because of his religious belief?" Waite's answer was no. "To permit this would be to make the professed doctrines of religious belief superior to the law of the land, and in effect to permit every citizen to become a law unto himself."

The 1890 case, coming out of Idaho, concerned a voter, Samuel D. Davis, who had falsely sworn that he was neither a polygamist, a bigamist, nor a member of any institution that sanctioned such marital arrangements. The Court unanimously agreed not only was Davis guilty of lying under oath but also that bigamy and polygamy were crimes in all "civilized and Christian countries." Justice Stephen J. Field, in addition to treating civilization and Christianity as virtually one and the same, viewed the advocacy or encouragement of polygamy as just as much a crime as the practice of it. This obscured the simple distinction in the earlier case between "mere opinion" and "subversive" behavior. Field also appealed not so much to constitutional language or even to legislative action as to "the moral judgment of the community" and "the common sense of mankind." Indeed, the moral judgment against polygamy in the United States was so pervasive and so deeply held that not until the Mormon Church explicitly rejected that practice could Utah be admitted into the Union, an event that took place in 1896.

In the 19th century, then, federal attention to First Amendment religion cases was quite limited. Before many decades had passed, however, this situation would change dramatically.

Supreme Court Decision:
Davis v. *Beason*

Samuel Davis of Idaho was accused of falsely swearing that he was neither a bigamist nor a polygamist. The Idaho court upheld that the territory had the right to deny Davis his voting privilages on this basis, and on appeal the U.S. Supreme Court concurred. A portion of the opinion, delivered by Justice Stephen J. Field in 1890, follows.

Bigamy and polygamy are crimes by the laws of the civilized and Christian countries. They are crimes by the laws of the United States, and they are crimes by the laws of Idaho. They tend to destroy the purity of the marriage relation, to disturb the peace of families, to degrade woman and to debase man. Few crimes are more pernicious to the best interests of society and receive more general or more deserved punishment. To extend exemption from punishment for such crimes would be to shock the moral judgment of the community. To call their advocacy a tenet of religion is to offend the common sense of mankind. If they are crimes, then to teach, advise and counsel their practice is to aid in their commission, and such teaching and counseling are themselves criminal and proper subjects of punishment, as aiding and abetting crime are in all other cases. . . .

It is assumed by counsel of the petitioner [Samuel D. Davis] that, because no mode of worship can be established or religious tenets enforced in this country, therefore any form of worship may be followed and any tenets, however destructive of society, may be held and advocated, if asserted to be part of the religious doctrine of those advocating and practicing them. But nothing is further from the truth. Whilst legislation for the establishment of a religion is forbidden, and its free exercise permitted, it does not follow that everything which may be so called can be tolerated. Crime is not the less odious because sanctioned by what any particular sect may designate as religion.

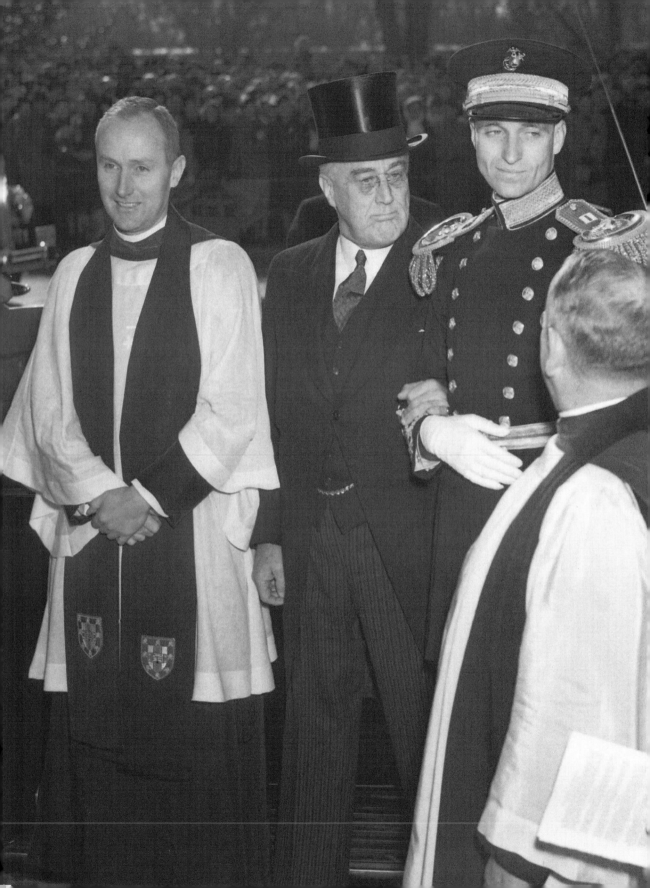

Chapter 4

The 20th Century and Beyond: A Busy Court

n the 19th century the U.S. Supreme Court heard relatively few church-state cases. During the 20th century, this changed dramatically, due to several factors.

First, the Court began (during the 1940s) to use the Fourteenth Amendment as a means of applying the First Amendment's religion clauses to the states. This change sharply increased the number of religion cases the Court could accept for review. Thus a trickle of church-state cases was transformed into a mighty river.

Second, many new organizations began challenging traditional religious practices in the public arena, again and again carrying the legal process all the way to the Supreme Court. At least three such groups deserve mention: the American Civil Liberties Union, the American Jewish Congress, and Americans United for Separation of Church and State. These groups carry on a kind of dialogue with the federal courts, testing how far religious liberty can be carried, or how near to religious establishment the government can come.

Third, the growth of religious pluralism throughout the nation means that religiously homogeneous communities are rapidly becoming a thing of the past. During the first half of the 19th century, many thought of the United States as predominantly a Protestant nation. Large-scale immigration, notably of Roman Catholics from Ireland and Jews from Eastern Europe, changed all that by the end of World War I. By the end of the 20th century, a "Judeo-Christian nation" had also to some degree become a Muslim, Buddhist, and totally pluralistic nation. Longstanding customs or practices could no longer be justified on the basis of tradition. Now they must be defended on constitutional grounds in order to survive.

Fourth, the federal government has become vastly larger and more intrusive than in the days of Jefferson or Jackson, Grant or Cleveland. Even such intimate matters as birth control, abortion, and sexual orientation have become, to one degree or another, federal questions. This being the case, the church and the state have more and more difficulty maintaining clear lines of separation.

And finally, the United States has become in recent years a society prone to sue or go to court over any number of issues—some serious and some trivial. In 1995, *U.S. News and World Report* described America as "the world's most litigious society," noting that in New York City alone more than a million lawsuits are filed in a single year. One result of this eagerness to sue is that the cost of liability insurance has soared beyond reasonable limits. Many doctors, for example, have stopped delivering babies either because they fear being sued or because the cost of medical malpractice insurance has risen far too high. In 1995, it took the profits from 87,000 boxes of Girl Scout cookies to cover that organization's liability insurance—even though the Girl Scouts had never been sued. Of course, the vast majority of liability cases never reaches the Supreme Court, but that Court, too, found itself more besieged in the 1980s and 1990s than ever before.

All these factors help explain why the Supreme Court is far busier today with religious questions than it was a century ago. They also help explain why in modern church-state cases the Court is so often divided in its judgments. When the decisions of the nine justices fail to be unanimous, it is a good guess that the American public has also had trouble reaching a consensus.

Although the Constitution prohibits any religious tests for federal offices, many states continued to impose such tests upon their publicly

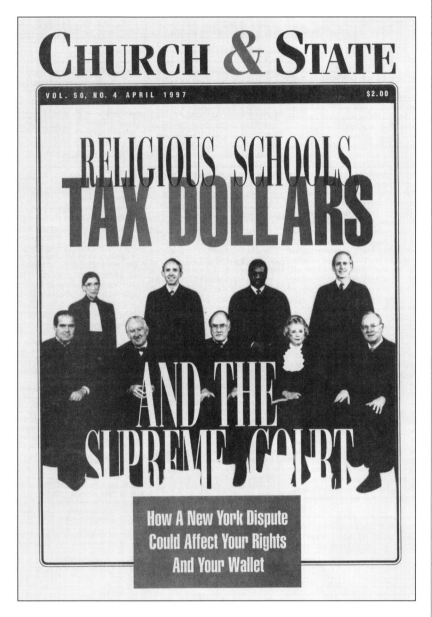

CHURCH & STATE

VOL. 50, NO. 4 APRIL 1997 $2.00

RELIGIOUS SCHOOLS
TAX DOLLARS
AND THE
SUPREME COURT

How A New York Dispute
Could Affect Your Rights
And Your Wallet

This monthly magazine is a publication of Americans United for Separation of Church and State. Organized in 1947, the group now boasts more than 50,000 members with representation in all 50 states.

elected officials. Often these tests were quite explicit, to the point of requiring an affirmation of belief in the Old and New Testaments and in an afterlife that included rewards and punishments. During the 19th century, most of these tests gradually faded away or were not enforced. The state of Maryland, however, retained the requirement of "a declaration of

During World War II, one function of the Medical Cadet Corps was to train conscientious objectors as medical personnel. Such objections to war were usually based on religious beliefs.

belief in the existence of God" by every official in the state. In the late 1950s, when Roy Torcaso sought a commission as a notary public, he was turned away because he, as an atheist, declined to take the oath. After failing to find relief in the Maryland courts, he took his case to the Supreme Court in 1961.

In *Torcaso* v. *Watkins,* the Court agreed that Maryland had violated Torcaso's First Amendment rights. "We repeat and again reaffirm," said Justice Hugo Black for the entire Court, that "neither a State nor the Federal Government can constitutionally force a person 'to profess a belief or a disbelief in any religion.'" Black also pointed out that a state could not discriminate between religions that taught belief in God and those, such as Buddhism and Taoism, that did not. He concluded that the Maryland religious test for public office "unconstitutionally invades the appellant's freedom of belief and religion and therefore cannot be enforced against him."

In 1978 the Court considered—in *McDaniel* v. *Paty*—the plight of a man excluded from public office not because he had too little religion but because he had too much: that is, he was a clergyman. The constitution of the state of Tennessee included a provision that prevented clergymen from serving in the legislature. Seven of the original 13 states, fearing too much political power in the hands of the clergy, had put similar provisions in their constitutions, though only Tennessee still retained such a prohibition.

The Court's majority found the restriction to be an infringement on the "free exercise of religion," for if one freely exercised his right to be a minister, he then incurred the burden of being barred from office. To that degree, his "free exercise" was manifestly less free. And the Court took comfort in the fact that James Madison had long before argued against such burdens because they punished a religious profession by denying a civil right. Also, this was a "religious test" just as surely as if Tennessee had declared that one must be a Baptist or Lutheran or Roman Catholic in order to serve in the legislature. (There were no dissenting opinions in this case, but several concurring opinions; that is, one or more justices agreed with the majority decision but presented a different line of argument for reaching the same conclusion.)

These two cases were decided with relative ease. More problematic were questions involving pacifists: those who, on grounds of religious conviction or conscience, objected to war and especially objected to bearing arms. Throughout U.S. history, conscientious objection has always been recognized within certain legislative or judicial limits. Until the 1960s, such objection always had a clear religious base. During World War I, for example, the Selective Service Draft Act (1917) provided an exemption from military service for members "of any well-recognized sect or organization . . . whose existing creed or principles forbid its members to participate in war in any form." Similar exemption was offered in World War II in the Selective Service Act (1940) to anyone "who, by reason of religious training and belief, is conscientiously opposed to war in any form."

During the long Vietnam War (1965–73), which grew increasingly unpopular, conscientious objection took some different turns that required the involvement of the Supreme Court in 1965, 1970, and again in 1971. These Court cases raised questions not directly confronted before. For example, what is religion? What is the meaning of the term *conscientious*? Can one conscientiously object only to a particular war, and can this objection be based on grounds other than religion? Finally, how does one fairly balance the national interest against the free exercise of religion? Answers did not come easily, and when they did come, it was not with the clarity and consistency for which many had hoped.

In *U.S.* v. *Seeger* (1965), the Court considered the case of Daniel Seeger, a young man from New York who claimed exemption from military service as a conscientious objector. Seeger's objection, however, was not based on his belief in a Supreme Being—a question that he preferred to leave open—but on his reading of many major works in ethics and philosophy. (Between 1948 and 1965, Congress had defined "religious training and belief" as meaning belief "in a Supreme Being.") Seeger stated that he held a "belief and devotion to goodness and virtue for their own sakes." Even though his belief was found to be sincere and honest, the draft board denied him the status of a conscientious objector because that belief did not rest upon traditional religious teachings, such as those associated with the historic "peace churches" of the Quakers and Mennonites. The New York courts had upheld the draft board's ruling.

The Supreme Court, on the other hand, took the "Supreme Being" language of the Congress in a broader sense than had formerly been the case. In the words of Justice William O. Douglas, "I agree with the Court that any person opposed to war on the basis of a sincere belief, which in his life fills the same place as a belief in God in the life of an orthodox religionist, is entitled to exemption under the statute." After this unanimous decision, reached in 1965, Congress dropped the requirement that one must believe in a Supreme Being in order to claim conscientious objector status. Congress retained, however, the phrase "by reason of religious training and belief" as necessary for making a valid objection to military service.

In *Welsh* v. *U.S.* (1970), the Court continued to take a broad view of the grounds upon which one might conscientiously object to war in general, or even to a particular war: namely, the Vietnam War. Elliott A. Welsh of California had been sentenced to three years in prison after refusing to be inducted into the armed forces of the United States. On the basis of the *Seeger* case, legal experts assumed that the decision of the California court would be reversed on appeal. And so it was. But this time the Supreme Court was divided 5 to 3, with the three dissenters emphasizing that Welsh's claim was based on "a purely personal code arising not from religious training and belief but from readings in philosophy, history, and sociology." The dissenters also pointed out that the Court's duty was "to enforce the will of Congress, not our own." Although Welsh received his exemption, the justices were clearly growing more uncomfortable with their "generous" interpretation of congressional intent.

Elliot A. Welsh talked enthusiastically to newsmen after the Supreme Court ruled that conscientious objection did not require a religious foundation. Cases such as these aroused great interest in the nation.

The following year, in *Gillette* v. *U.S.*, the Court swung back to a far more conservative position. Objections to a particular war, said the Court, are more likely to be political and not based on a religiously informed conscience. Furthermore, the courts were obliged to make certain that those who are drafted for military service are not "chosen unfairly or capriciously." For should that even appear to be the case, "then a mood of bitterness and cynicism might corrode the spirit of public service." By a vote of 8 to 1, the Court decided that Guy P. Gillette would not be exempted from military service because Gillette objected not to "war in any form," as congressional language stipulated, but only to one particular war, namely that in Vietnam. After all, the Court concluded, the U.S. Constitution did not provide for conscientious objection to war; it was a congressional grace rather than a constitutional right.

The one dissenter, William O. Douglas, acknowledged that the Constitution did not speak precisely to the point of conscientious objection to war. "Yet conscience and belief are the main ingredients of First Amendment rights," Douglas added. But his was a lone voice. In the space of six years, the Court moved from a unanimous opinion that was broad and liberal, to a divided opinion that was broad but hesitant, to a virtually unanimous opinion that returned to the restrictions that Congress had earlier laid down. In the area of conscientious objection to all war or any war, the direction set down by the Court in these three cases has been less than convincing or clear.

Questions of conscience are, by their nature, quite agonizing for all concerned. And no matters of conscience appear more sensitive or more delicate that those pertaining to birth control and abortion. Although, strictly speaking, these are not questions of church and state, the fact remains that churches are heavily involved in lobbying—on both sides—of the strong and passionate arguments. For its part, the state might prefer to leave these matters as purely personal, essentially private decisions. But a variety of municipal and state laws, as well as issues of federal funding, make this strategic withdrawal impossible. So the courts, no less than the churches, find themselves obliged to speak.

In 1965 the U.S. Supreme Court turned its attention to a Connecticut law of 1879 that made it a crime for any person to utilize a drug, article, or instrument to interfere with or prevent conception. It was also deemed criminal to disseminate information about birth control techniques, even to married couples. The explicit language of the First Amendment did not directly address the issue at hand, so Justice William O. Douglas, writing for the majority, looked for implications in the Bill of Rights and the Fourteenth Amendment that would give the Court some basis for action. He found it in the shadows of these amendments: namely, a right to privacy. The Ninth Amendment in particular, Justice Arthur J. Goldberg wrote in a concurring opinion, authorizes the Court to identify additional liberties, especially when they are "so rooted in the traditions and conscience of our people as to be ranked fundamental." So by a vote of 7 to 2, the Court (in *Griswold* v. *Connecticut*) found the Connecticut law invalid with respect to the birth

Supreme Court Decision:
Roe v. *Wade,* 1972

Justice Harry Blackmun introduced his lengthy decision with words that recognized the enormous complexity of the case before the Court.

We forthwith acknowledge our awareness of the sensitive and emotional nature of the abortion controversy, of the vigorous opposing views, even among physicians, and of the deep and seemingly absolute convictions that the subject inspires. One's philosophy, one's experiences, one's exposure to the raw edges of human existence, one's religious training, one's attitude toward life and family and their values, and the moral standards one establishes and seeks to observe are all likely to influence and color one's thinking and conclusions about abortion.

In addition, population growth, pollution, poverty, and racial overtones tend to complicate and not to simplify the problem.

Our task, of course, is to resolves the issue by constitutional measurement, free of emotion and predilection. We seek earnestly to do this, and, because we do, we have inquired into, and in this opinion place some emphasis upon, medical and medical-legal history and what that history reveals about man's attitude toward the abortion procedure over the centuries.

We bear in mind, too, Mr. Justice Holmes' admonition in his now vindicated dissent in *Lochner* v. *New York,* 198 U.S. 45, 76 (1905): The Constitution is made for people of fundamentally differing views, and the accident of our finding certain opinions natural and familiar or novel and even shocking ought not to conclude our judgment upon the question whether statues embodying them conflict with the Constitution of the United States.

control practices of married couples. Seven years later, in *Eisenstadt* v. *Baird*, the Court extended the same privileges to unmarried persons.

But in that same year, 1972, it took on an even more intensely debated issue: the legality of illegality of abortion. In *Roe* v. *Wade* the Court (again in a 7 to 2 vote) spoke in words that have refused to die. In a long, carefully crafted opinion, Justice Harry Blackmun acknowledged the deep divisions within the American public. Those divisions had grown deeper in recent years as a result of greater sexual freedom and the increasing force of the women's movement. Moreover, the enormous variety of abortion laws among the states meant that some women, able to afford travel to states where abortions were legal, could obtain the procedure legally and under sanitary conditions, while poorer women were often subjected to unsafe "back-alley" operations. Protests against abortion laws were regularly declared moot, since by the time a case reached the relevant court the pregnancy had already been terminated or the baby had been born. By 1971, however, the Supreme Court decided that a case needed to be heard whether or not a specific pregnancy was still pending.

So in 1971, and then again the following year, it at last heard cases involving antiabortion laws in the state of Texas. The Court handed down its decision on January 22, 1973. The specific date is worth mentioning because January 22 has become an annual commemoration of "Human Sanctity" by the "right to life" forces, with counter demonstrations led by those identified as "pro-choice." Each side sees *Roe* v. *Wade* as the focal point—a judicial decision to be overturned at almost any cost, or to be defended with similar intensity.

In his opinion, Blackmun reviewed in detail the history of abortion practices around the world, and the arguments (legal, moral, and religious) offered in support of or in opposition to such varied practices. Then, drawing on the right to privacy spelled out several years earlier (in *Griswold)*, Blackmun argued that antiabortion laws violated that right. But he also conceded that state has a legitimate interest in regulating the right to an abortion. In an effort to balance these competing interests, Blackmun distinguished between the three trimesters of a normal nine-month pregnancy. In the first three months, the woman, in consultation with her physician, could ascertain the appropriateness of an abortion. In the second three months, states could regulate abortions to protect the health of the mother. And in the final three months, the rights of the fetus must be taken into consideration, so that abortion could be justified only if the life of the mother were threatened.

The two dissenters, William Rehnquist and Byron White, complained in separate opinions that the Court was guaranteeing a right nowhere spelled out in the Constitution. Moreover, they said, the rights of the fetus deserved to be protected throughout the pregnancy, not just in the last three months. And if one is tempted to say that "there the matter rested," the facts cry out otherwise.

In 1989 and again in 1992, cases from Missouri and Pennsylvania required a reexamination of some aspects of the 1973 decision. And one point is immediately obvious: the Court moved from a 7 to 2 vote in *Roe* v. *Wade* to 5 to 4 votes in both of the later cases. Opponents of *Roe* held their collective breath, hoping that it would be overturned; supporters of *Roe* likewise held their collective breath hoping that it would be sustained—as it very narrowly was. The Missouri case, *Webster* v. *Reproductive Services* (1989), gave the Court a chance to bow out of the turbulent field entirely, returning all abortion matters to the states. But that the Court declined to do. Missouri could further restrict access to abortions, but it could it could not prohibit such access altogether. *Roe* was not overturned. The Pennsylvania case, *Planned Parenthood* v. *Casey* (1992), found the Court even more divided than the 5 to 4 vote indicated. Two justices (Stevens and Blackmun) wanted the Pennsylvania laws voided altogether; four justices (Rehnquist, Scalia, White, Thomas) wanted *Roe* voided altogether. A center coalition of David Souter, Sandra Day O'Connor, and Arthur Kennedy made the difference in keeping *Roe* alive—but barely.

The three "centrists" recognized that, in the words of Sandra Day O'Connor, "Men and women of good conscience can disagree, and we suppose some always shall disagree, about the profound moral and spiritual implications of terminating a pregnancy, even in its earliest stages." Even the Supreme Court, as the vote tally made obvious, came to contrary conclusions. But, the three jurists declared, "Our obligation is to

In Milwaukee, Wisconsin, pro-life activist Jan Parshall (left) and pro-choice supporter Maggi Cage work together to assist pregnant women.

define the liberty of all, not to mandate our own moral code." Chief Justice William Rehnquist argued in dissent that the Court was giving too much attention to public opinion and public pressures. "The Judicial Branch," he noted, "derives its legitimacy, not from following public opinion, but from deciding by its best lights whether legislative enactments of the popular branches of Government comport with the Constitution." And by those "best lights," Rehnquist concluded that the Pennsylvania laws should be upheld and Roe overturned.

The Court had spoken, but not with a definitiveness or finality that many had sought. Deep disagreements remained, and if they could not be resolved in the courts, perhaps they could be resolved in the streets. Demonstrations against abortion clinics and abortion providers led in extreme cases to bombings and killings. In some states, laws permitting abortions became meaningless since no doctors remained to provide them. Courts found it necessary to provide "buffer zones" around abortion clinics, allowing demonstrations to continue but forbidding the blocking of access to the clinics' services. In several states, a late-term abortion procedure, variously designated dilation and extraction or "partial birth" abortion, was prohibited by laws often so vague as to make many doctors wary of any and all procedures for terminating a pregnancy. A federal law banning such procedures was vetoed by President Clinton in 1999, and Congress failed to override his veto. The House, however, has almost on an annual basis continued to pass a bill outlawing this late-term procedure, though the Senate has thus far failed to follow suit.

On both the state and federal levels the question of parental consent for a teenager's abortion was repeatedly raised. And in the U.S. Congress foreign aid bills were delayed or tabled until agreements could be reached on the use of any federal funds for abortions, including among the U.S. military serving abroad. In the brief period from 1996 to 1999 nearly a hundred abortion-related votes came before Congress in what many saw as an effort gradually to whittle away at the effect of *Roe* v. *Wade*. In the twenty-first century, with churches divided, with courts unclear, and with American society in continual turmoil, one searches in vain for any sign of a swift or satisfying resolution.

Other church-state questions may seem less agonizing: for example, the display of nativity scenes at Christmastime on public property. Yet these cases have given the Court considerable difficulty and created sharp divisions. In Pawtucket, Rhode Island, the city government had for more than 40 years paid for an annual Christmas season display that included the nativity scene. This display, placed in the shopping district, also featured a Santa Claus house, a sleigh pulled by cutout figures of reindeer, candy-striped poles, carolers, and hundreds of colored lights. Some Pawtucket citizens, assisted by the American Civil Liberties Union, objected to the use of city funds for religious displays. The church-state question was, of course, confined to the crèche, or nativity scene, but the entire context in which it appeared was relevant to the Court's 1984 decision in *Lynch* v. *Donnelly*.

That decision turned out to be a difficult one, for the Court was divided as severely as nine justices can be: 5 to 4. The bare majority, with Chief Justice Warren Burger as its spokesman, upheld the right of Pawtucket to

Supreme Court Decision:
Lynch v. Donnelly

In the 1984 case of Lynch v. Donnelly, *Justice Sandra Day O'Connor issued a separate concurring opinion, that is, an opinion that agreed with the Court's decision but offered other arguments for reaching that conclusion. A portion of her opinion follows.*

The Establishment Clause prohibits government from making adherence to a religion relevant in any way to a person's standing in the political community. Government can run afoul of that prohibition in two principal ways. One is excessive entanglement with religious institutions, which may interfere with the independence of religious institutions, give the institutions access to government or governmental powers not fully shared by nonadherents of the religion, and foster the creation of political constituencies defined along religious lines. . . . The second and more direct infringement is government endorsement or disapproval of religion. Endorsement sends a message to nonadherents that they are outsiders, not full members of the political community, and an accompanying message to adherents that they are insiders, favored members of the political community. Disapproval sends the opposite message. . . .

Pawtucket's display of its crèche, I believe, does not communicate a message that the government intends to endorse the Christian beliefs represented by the crèche. Although the religious and indeed sectarian significance of the crèche, as the District Court found, is not neutralized by the setting, the overall holiday setting changes what viewers may fairly understand to be the purpose of the display—as a typical museum setting, though not neutralizing the religious content of a religious painting, negates any message of endorsement of that content. The display celebrates a public holiday, and no one contends that declaration of that holiday is understood to be an endorsement of religion. The holiday itself has very strong secular components and traditions. Government celebration of the holiday, which is extremely common, generally is not understood to endorse the religious content of the holiday, just as government celebration of Thanksgiving is not so understood. The crèche is a traditional symbol of the holiday that is very commonly displayed along with purely secular symbols, as it was in Pawtucket.

sponsor and support the Christmas display. The crèche, the majority asserted, must be viewed in the context of the entire Christmas scene, which, when taken as a whole, did not constitute "some kind of subtle governmental advocacy of a particular religious message." If there was some benefit to a single faith or religion, that benefit was "indirect, remote, and incidental." Burger found the nativity display to be "no more an advancement or endorsement of religion than the Congressional and Executive recognition of the origins of the Holiday itself as 'Christ's Mass.'"

The four dissenters judged otherwise. With Justice William Brennan as their spokesman, they noted that if this case appeared hard, it was only "because the Christmas holiday seems so familiar and agreeable." But that familiarity must not be allowed to obscure "the plain fact that Pawtucket's action amounts to an impermissible governmental endorsement of a particular faith." Brennan noted that way back in 1892 a justice of the Supreme Court "arrogantly" declared that "this is a Christian nation" (*Church of the Holy Trinity* v. *U.S.*). But, said Brennan, "those days, I had thought, were forever put behind us." Clearly, they are not behind us, Brennan concluded, when a majority of the Court fails to recognize the city's action for what it is: "a coercive, though perhaps small, step toward establishing the sectarian preferences of the majority at the expense of the minority."

Five-to-four decisions are notoriously slippery: that is, they do not establish solid precedents upon which to build. Five years later, the Court considered a similar case from Pittsburgh, Pennsylvania. Here, an outdoor display featured an 18-foot menorah commemorating the Jewish holiday of Hanukkah and a 45-foot-tall decorated Christmas tree. Inside, on the main staircase of the Allegheny County Courthouse, a crèche, donated by a Roman Catholic group, was displayed. The American Civil Liberties Union sued the county on the grounds that this display violated the separation of church and state. This complex case (*County of Allegheny* v. *Greater Pittsburgh American Civil Liberties Union*, 1989) produced an opinion of more than 100 pages that revealed a much-divided, much-perturbed Supreme Court.

Six justices agreed that the outdoor display (menorah and tree) was permissible because it was "not an endorsement of religious faith but simply a recognition of cultural diversity." Five justices, on the other hand, found that the inside display of the crèche had a clear sectarian purpose. For one thing, it stood alone: no Santa Claus, sleigh, striped candy poles, or reindeer (which led some cynics to refer to the "reindeer rule" in deciding whether a nativity scene was allowable or not). For another thing, the crèche bore a banner with the Latin words *Gloria in Excelsis Deo* (Glory to God in the Highest). For these reasons, said Justice Harry Blackmun for the majority, the religious message and religious intent of the crèche were clear. The Court, therefore, upheld "the long-standing constitutional principle that government may not engage in a practice that has the effect of promoting or endorsing religious beliefs."

But four justices thought that both displays were constitutionally acceptable. Writing for this minority, Justice Anthony Kennedy, in a spirited dissent, saw no element of coercion in the "passive symbols" of the menorah or the crèche. "Passersby who disagree with the message conveyed by these displays are free to ignore them, or even to turn their backs." What he did find in the majority opinion was a "callous indifference" to religion, if not a hostility as well. "I would be the first to admit that many questions arising under the Establishment Clause do not admit of easy answers," Kennedy added, "but whatever the Clause requires, it is not the result reached by the Court today."

Obviously, the U.S. Supreme Court can argue as vigorously with itself as it may with the rulings of lower courts. Moreover, the two religion clauses of the First Amendment do not by themselves settle every church-state issue. Often, they simply become the point of departure for lines of reasoning and arguments that lead some justices in one direction and other justices down a different road.

Sometimes the Court is obliged to balance the two religion clauses against each other. For example, the federal government pays military chaplains who serve in the armed forces. Does that not sound like an endorsement of and support for religion and therefore a violation of the establishment clause? On the other hand, failure to provide such chaplains would surely interfere with the free exercise of religion on the part of military personnel stationed far from home or on foreign soil. In this

case there is a need for balance: the claims of free exercise against the dangers of establishment. And most Americans seem content to let this arrangement continue, without any serious legal challenge being made.

What about chaplains hired by and for the U.S. Congress, or chaplains hired with state funds for their own legislative assemblies? Here the issue may not be quite so clear-cut. James Madison, for example, argued long ago that if Congress needed a pastor, then it could do what all of its constituents were obliged to do: namely, hire one on their own, and pay for him or her out of their own pockets. Besides, he noted, the whole ritual of prayers at the opening of congressional sessions had become a "tiresome formality"; few bothered to attend. Madison's views on this issue were not persuasive in the early 19th century, nor have they proved very persuasive since his time.

The Supreme Court, however, did agree to hear a case coming out of Nebraska in 1983 (*Marsh* v. *Chambers*). The state of Nebraska had hired a

This nativity scene in Pawtucket, Rhode Island, was ruled permissible by a Supreme Court vote of 5-4. Split votes are notoriously weak and encourage challenges.

A regimental chaplain holds a Jewish service in an orchard in Normandy during World War II. The Ten Commandments and a Star of David adorn the military jeep behind him.

chaplain, whose duties included opening every legislative session with prayer. One member of the legislature, Ernest Chambers, objected to this arrangement, which he saw as a violation of the establishment clause. A federal district court concluded that the prayers were acceptable but that paying a chaplain with state funds was not. The U.S. Court of Appeals then ruled that the whole arrangement was unconstitutional, whereupon the state of Nebraska appealed to the Supreme Court.

By a vote of 6 to 3, the Supreme Court ruled that the Nebraska pattern did not violate the establishment clause of the First Amendment. Chief Justice Warren Burger, speaking for the majority, explained: "To invoke Divine guidance on a public body entrusted with making the laws is not, in these circumstances, an 'establishment' of religion." Burger added that "it is simply a tolerable acknowledgment of beliefs widely held among the people of this country." Burger also appealed to the unbroken tradition of more than two centuries of prayers being offered by paid chaplains in the U.S. Congress. Such practice, he observed, "is deeply embedded in the history and tradition of this country."

The dissenters did not find the lessons of history similarly persuasive. Indeed, said Justice William Brennan on their behalf, "the Court's focus here on a narrow piece of history is, in a fundamental sense, a betrayal of history." The Constitution "is not a static document whose meaning on every detail is fixed for all time by the life experience of the Framers." Likewise, the members of the 1st Congress "should be treated, not as sacred figures whose every action must be emulated, but as the authors of a [Bill of Rights] meant to last for the ages." Brennan conceded that if the Court had struck down the practice of legislative chaplains, "it would likely have stimulated a furious reaction." But, he countered, "it would also, I am convinced, have invigorated both the 'spirit of religion' and the 'spirit of freedom.'"

Finally, there is one issue that affects every religious institution in the nation: the exemption of church property from taxation. Because every city or county in the United States is concerned with raising revenues, it might be supposed that many local authorities would challenge the churches' tax-exempt status. However, there is a long tradition of granting such exemptions that dates back to the Roman Emperor Constantine, who made Christianity the official religion of the Roman Empire in 325 and decreed that churches would not be taxed. This same precedent prevailed in North America from the very beginning of the colonial settlements. The historical tradition is often bolstered by the argument that churches (along with schools, hospitals, and many charities) perform valuable services that the government would otherwise have to undertake. Nonetheless, some might question whether churches have an unfair advantage, or whether present practices are constitutionally correct. Is a grant of tax exemption the equivalent of a grant of money? And if so, is that not a violation of the establishment clause of the First Amendment?

In *Walz* v. *Tax Commission of the City of New York* (1970), the Supreme Court at last addressed these and other questions. Frederick

THE RELIGION BU$INESS

ALFRED BALK

Many people (including James Madison) feared that the churches' tax-exempt status would result in their acquiring great wealth. This satiric cartoon contrasts the rich, indifferent church with the humble, impoverished Jesus.

Walz, a lawyer who owned a small parcel of land on Staten Island, contended that he was being asked to subsidize the churches—if they were taxed, his tax bill would be smaller. Though the money in question may have been trifling—Walz paid only $5.40 a year in property tax—the principle was large, involving both clauses of the First Amendment and the proper balance between them.

Chief Justice Burger, speaking for the majority (there was only a single dissent), noted that "the Court has struggled to find a neutral course between the two Religion Clauses, both of which are cast in absolute terms, and either of which, if expanded to a logical extreme, would tend to clash with the other." Between these two absolutes, Burger argued, one could find "some room for play in the joints" and emerge with a "benevolent neutrality" that "simply abstains from demanding that the church support the state."

The chief justice also appealed to history, noting an earlier justice's comment that "a page of history is worth a volume of logic." In 200 years of U.S. history, Burger noted, this tax exemption had not "given the remotest sign" of leading to an established church. "On the contrary," Burger concluded, "it has operated affirmatively to help guarantee the free exercise of all forms of religious belief." Moreover, while even tax exemption leads to some necessary contact between the church and the state, the process of tax collecting would lead to vastly more contact—an "excessive entanglement" that the Court specifically sought to avoid.

The single dissenter, Justice William O. Douglas, argued at some length that tax exemption was a subsidy, whether one wished to call it that or not. If we are going to appeal to history, Douglas argued, let us then acknowledge that the exemptions are merely a holdover from the days of official established churches. "If believers are entitled to public financial support, so are nonbelievers," Douglas wrote. "For one of the mandates of the First Amendment [is] to promote a viable, pluralistic society, and to keep government neutral." To drive his point home, Douglas appended to his opinion the Patrick Henry bill proposing the establishment of Christianity in Virginia, and James Madison's *Memorial and Remonstrance,* written in opposition to that proposal.

The American public at large may not get deeply involved in questions of religious tests, legislative chaplains, nativity scenes, or even tax exemptions. But the field of education, both public and private, is one that touches nearly everyone's life. Here there is widespread public involvement and deep national concern.

A In *Adam's* Fall
We Sinned all.

B Thy Life to Mend
This *Book* Attend.

C The *Cat* doth play
And after slay.

D A *Dog* will bite
A Thief at night.

E An *Eagles* flight
Is out of sight.

F The Idle *Fool*
Is whipt at School.

Chapter 5

The Establishment Clause: Public Schools

n Western civilization, the connection between religion and education is both intimate and of long duration. When an imperial state controlled the church, it also controlled the educational system. And when, as on occasion in the Middle Ages the church dominated the state, it dominated the schools and universities as well. Even in the modern world, in most European nations the ties between state education and institutional religion remain close. But not in the United States of America.

In U.S. public schools, where the vast majority of the nation's young people are educated, control tends to be local rather than federal. And in those schools the constitutionally correct way of dealing with (or ignoring) religion tends to be a major problem for all concerned: the pupils, the parents, the religious leaders, the school teachers and administrators, and the political leadership at all governmental levels. Perhaps it is not surprising that problems arise, because the U.S. experiment in education swims against such a strong historical tide in the Western world.

When Horace Mann, a Massachusetts lawyer and legislator, reformed the public school system of his state in the late 1830s and early 1840s, he set an example that was followed by many other states. Gradually, most states adopted laws making education compulsory through age 16 or through a certain grade level, though such laws did not become universal until the 20th century.

the 18th century, *The w England Primer* taught ʌerican children their letʌs. In addition, it taught ʌders their place in the ʌial and religious order, ʌnsmitting values of ʌponsibility, piety, modʌy, and obedience.

Archbishop John Hughes led the campaign for parochial schools in New York. He then fought, and eventually lost, the battle for public monies for religious schools.

Mann also set a pattern by excluding "all dogmatical theology and sectarianism" from public school instruction. This, however, did not mean that public schools were free of nondogmatic Protestantism. Pupils sang Protestant hymns, read from a Protestant Bible (King James Version), offered Protestant prayers, and read their history with a strongly Protestant (that is to say, anti-Catholic) slant. Indeed, Archbishop John Hughes in New York City thought the public schools in the 1840s were so clearly Protestant that public monies should be granted to Roman Catholic schools as well. When he failed to win that argument, he turned to what seemed the only alternative: a parochial school system for Catholic boys and girls.

As early as 1869, parents sued the public schools of Cincinnati, Ohio, in an effort to purge them of their Protestant religious exercises. The Superior Court of that city, more or less in the spirit of Horace Mann, found nothing objectionable in these "non-dogmatic," yet clearly Protestant, observances. One dissenter, however, Judge Alphonso Taft (father of future President William Howard Taft) noted that these daily rituals were clearly "Protestant worship" and, as such, inescapably "offensive to Catholics and Jews." A year later, the Ohio Supreme Court agreed with Taft's dissenting opinion and ruled such activity illegal. Nevertheless, a century later the U.S. Supreme Court found itself wrestling with quite similar issues, as did the U.S. Congress. A large part of the difficulty could be traced to that persistent Protestant flavor, in one section of the country or another, in the locally controlled public school system.

Following World War II, public school cases reached the Supreme Court in large numbers. With the First Amendment's establishment clause now made applicable to the states, the question arose repeatedly whether any governmental agency—federal, state, or local—was engaged in an endorsement or support of religion. And in these cases, the Court showed special sensitivity to the vulnerability or susceptibility of the young while showing less concern about ritual or symbolism affecting the populace at large. For example, the Court has steadily declined to hear any case objecting to the presence of "In God We Trust" on some of the nation's coins. This practice, dating back to the dark days of the Civil War, received congressional sanction in 1865. President Theodore Roosevelt dropped the motto in 1905, not on the grounds of separation of church and state but largely because, in his opinion, it "cheapened" the sanctity of religion. Congress addressed the issue in 1908, making the motto mandatory on certain gold and silver coins. "In God We Trust" remains, objected to by a few, ignored by most.

Horace Mann, a lawyer and legislator, forged the model for public school education. He saw nothing wrong with a non-sectarian (that is, vaguely Protestant) presence in the public schools.

The public school cases discussed in this chapter fall into four distinct categories: (1) those that involve teaching of religion in some fashion or other on the school grounds ("released time"), off the school grounds ("dismissed time"), or in cooperation with a parochial school ("shared time"); (2) the actual practice of religion in the public schools (prayers, Bible reading, hymns, and even services of worship); (3) questions associated with the teaching of certain subjects that may be thought of as more religious than academic in nature; (4) the right of students to engage in religious practices in school buildings, or on school grounds.

With respect to the first category, the Supreme Court in 1948 heard its initial case concerning a portion of the school day being given over to sectarian religious instruction. This case, *McCollum* v. *Board of Education*, arose in Champaign, Illinois, where since 1940 the schools had set aside 45 minutes during the week so that pastors, priests, or rabbis could visit the schools and offer instruction to those of their respective faiths.

Although many people view it as such, the balance is not actually between "atheism" and the Bible, but between the demands of the First Amendment and the desires of the religious population.

Students who chose no sectarian class were placed in a regular class or a study hall. The Court, by a vote of 8 to 1, found this "released time" plan to be unconstitutional.

In a concurring opinion, Justice Felix Frankfurter declared that "separation means separation, not something less." After citing Jefferson's reference to a "wall of separation," he observed that it should really be a wall, not "a fine line easily overstepped." The public school, Frankfurter added, "is at once the symbol of our democracy and the most pervasive means for promoting our common destiny." Therefore, one should strive to keep out that which would divide the students into separate groups. "If nowhere else," he concluded, "in the relation between Church and State, 'good fences make good neighbors.'" The single dissenter, Justice Stanley Reed, argued that the Constitution "should not be stretched to forbid national customs" or conflict with "accepted habits of our people." And with respect to the Jeffersonian "wall of separation" Reed observed that "a rule of law should not be drawn from a figure of speech."

Four years later, the Court agreed to hear a somewhat similar case coming out of New York City, *Zorach* v. *Clauson*. At this time, New York public schools dismissed their students early one day a week to go to the nearest church or synagogue to receive sectarian instruction. Those who chose not to participate remained in class until the regular school day was over. Because of many similarities with the *McCollum* case, it was widely predicted that the Court would also find the New York City arrangement to be unconstitutional. But, by a vote of 6 to 3, the Court upheld it.

The issue at stake in the *Zorach* case has been called "dismissed time" to distinguish it from the earlier "released time" plan. Here students were dismissed to attend their various religious institutions, and no clergy came to the public school or utilized any of its facilities. The public schools participated only to the extent of receiving attendance records from the clergy and reporting as truant those who stated they were going to religion classes but did not show up. A majority of the Court found dismissed time acceptable, Justice William Douglas declaring that when school authorities adjust "the schedule of public events to sectarian needs," they are then following "the best of our traditions." He added, "we find no constitutional requirement which makes it necessary for government to be hostile to religion."

The three dissenters disagreed so strongly with this reasoning that each of them wrote a separate opinion. Justice Robert Jackson's was the most vigorous, for he regarded the distinction between dismissed time and released time as "trivial, almost to the point of cynicism." "We start down a rough road," he noted, "when we begin to mix compulsory public education with compulsory godliness." Jackson also tried to make it clear that he bore no hostility toward religion, only hostility toward any compulsion in religion. "It is possible," he observed, "to hold a faith with enough confidence to believe that what should be rendered to God does not need to be decided and collected by Caesar."

A third method employed by some public and private schools was "shared time," whereby students could be taught both by parochial school teachers (subjects that might raise moral or theological questions, such as history, literature, and religion) and by public school teachers (less value-laden subjects such as mathematics, reading, and physical education). Addressing this issue in *Grand Rapids School District* v. *Ball* and *Aguilar* v. *Felton,* both cases heard in 1985, the Court was badly divided, but 5-to-4 majorities found shared time to be unconstitutional.

In the Grand Rapids case, Justice Brennan, speaking for the slim majority, objected that public school teachers offering instruction in a parochial school might give the impression that the state endorsed the school's religion: "The symbolism of a union between church and state is most likely to influence children of tender years." Apart from the symbolism, Brennan thought the arrangement constituted major financial assistance to the religious schools, who were utilizing teachers paid by the state. "To let the genie out of the bottle in this case would be to permit ever larger segments of the religious school curriculum to be turned over to the public school system." Were this to happen, Brennan concluded, we would violate "the cardinal principle that the State may not in effect become the prime supporter of the religious school system."

The four dissenters saw the majority opinion as just another in a long line of erroneous judgments. As Justice (later Chief Justice) William Rehnquist noted, so many of those bad judgments were based on the faulty premise of a Jeffersonian "wall." Moreover, Rehnquist saw in the majority opinion a basic distrust of the public school teachers' ability to separate secular and religious matters while teaching in parochial schools. He pointed out that the records of both the 1985 shared-time cases contained "not one instance of attempted religious inculcation [though] both programs have been in operation for a number of years."

As history has shown, cases decided by a 5-to-4 vote tend to be "slippery." After 12 years, the Rehnquist dissent led to another 5-to-4 vote with respect to shared time, but on this occasion the finding turned out to be favorable to New York's parochial schools. In the 1997 case, *Agostini* v. *Felton,* the Court overruled its 1985 decision in *Aguilar* v. *Felton.* Now public school teachers were permitted to teach remedial and supplemental classes to needy children *within* the parochial school. Writing for the majority of five, Justice Sandra Day O'Connor noted that "we no longer presume that public employees will inculcate religion simply because they happen to be in a sectarian environment." On behalf of the four dissenters, Justice David Souter observed that this new decision authorized "state aid to religious institutions on an unparalleled scale, in violation of the Establishment Clause's central prohibition against religious subsidies by the government."

A second category of public school cases related to actual acts of worship within the schools. In *Engel* v. *Vitale* (1962), the Court considered the constitutionality of a prayer that New York's State Board of Regents had mandated in all public school classrooms at the beginning of each school day. The prayer seemed inoffensive enough: "Almighty God, we acknowledge our dependence upon Thee, and we beg Thy blessings upon us, our parents, our teachers and our Country." But the question, of course, was whether it belonged in the public schools at the order of state agency.

With only a single dissent, the Court determined that this use of the Regents' prayer constituted "a practice wholly inconsistent with the Establishment Clause." Justice Hugo Black, on behalf of the Court, added: "The constitutional prohibition against laws respecting an establishment of religion must at least mean that in this country it is no part of the business of government to compose official prayers for any group of the American people to recite as a part of a religious program carried on by government." Black took note of the probable public reaction: namely, that the Court's decision would indicate "a hostility toward religion or toward prayer." But, said Black, nothing "could be more wrong." The authors of the First Amendment, he pointed out, tried to "put an end to governmental control of religion and prayer," but they did so with the conviction that "a union of government and religion tends to destroy government and degrade religion."

The lone dissenter, Justice Potter Stewart, argued that New York's practice did not even come close to an establishment of religion. The real

First graders share a moment of silent prayer at the start of their day in a South Carolina public school. The Supreme Court's 1962 decision not to allow state mandated prayer in the classroom enraged many Americans.

question was "whether school children who want to begin their day by joining in prayer must be prohibited from doing so." He added that the Regents' prayer, like a Presidential proclamation of a national day of prayer, simply recognized "the deeply entrenched and highly cherished spiritual traditions of our Nation." On the Court, Stewart's voice was a solitary one, but it soon became obvious that he spoke for a large segment of the general public.

Religious leaders, politicians, editorial writers, and many others attacked the Court with anger and abuse. The majority opinion was denounced as "asinine," "stupid," "appalling," and possibly Communist inspired. Evangelist Billy Graham said, "God pity our country when we can no longer appeal to God for help." And Francis Cardinal Spellman of New York declared, "This decision strikes at the very heart of the Godly tradition in which America's children have for so long been raised." Of course, many citizens weighed in on the other side, but not with equal volume. Reverend Martin Luther King, Jr. described the Court's decision as "sound and good, reaffirming something basic in the Nation's life: separation of church and state." President John F. Kennedy pointed out that the Court had done nothing to discourage prayer but rather returned it to its proper locale: the church and the home. The American Jewish Congress strongly supported the majority decision, as did the National Council of Churches and a large number of Protestant denominations.

The most far-reaching reaction, however, was in the Congress itself. There, from 1962 to the present, proposals have been offered to amend the Constitution in a manner that would nullify the Court's decision in *Engel* v. *Vitale*. Constitutional amendments require a two-thirds vote in both houses of Congress, then ratification by three-fourths of the states. This process, deliberately made difficult by the original framers, has not yet produced an amendment on school prayer, but successive Court decisions have assured that efforts to add one will continue.

In 1963, the Court rendered two opinions that further fanned the flames of opposition. A case from Pennsylvania (*Abingdon* v. *Schempp*) and one from Maryland (*Murray* v. *Curlett*) were decided together, for the Court saw the constitutional issue as the same. Daily devotional Bible reading and the recitation of the Lord's Prayer in public schools were the activities at issue here, and the Court (with Justice Stewart again as the single dissenter) found these to be in violation of the First Amendment, just as the Regents' prayer had been. To aid them in reaching a decision, the justices devised "tests" to determine whether legislation in the realm of church-state matters would be constitutional or not. The purpose and primary effect of any law must be secular, they maintained, neither advancing nor inhibiting religion. Daily Bible reading of 10 verses, without comment, had no secular purpose, the Justices argued, only a religious one. And the same was true of a ritualized recitation of the Lord's Prayer. This was clearly intended to advance religion and therefore was, just as clearly, a violation of the establishment clause.

That these exercises were voluntary—any student could be excused from them "upon the written request" of parent or guardian—was beside the

Madalyn Murray and her sons, William and Garth, leave the Supreme Court after it ruled that reciting the Lord's Prayer and the reading of the Bible in the classroom were unconstitutional. William was being raised an atheist.

point in the Court's judgment. Justice Tom Clark explained that coercion was an essential factor in a violation of the First Amendment's free-exercise clause; but with respect to the establishment clause, any governmental support or advancement of religion was prohibited, voluntary or not.

Mindful of the storm that had greeted the 1962 case, the Court tried to forestall such a reaction this time by making clear that the Court was not hostile to religion, not even hostile to religion in the public schools, just so long as it was a matter for *study* and not an act of *worship*. "It might well be said," the Court noted, "that one's education is not complete without a study of comparative religion or the history of religion and its relationship to the advancement of civilization." Beyond that, "It certainly may be said that the Bible is worthy of study for its literary and historic qualities." Nothing in the Court's decision today, Justice Clark emphasized, would prohibit such academic enterprises.

But this clear statement did little to mollify an already aroused public. Nor did Justice Stewart's dissent help the majority's case, for he attacked the "sterile metaphor" of a wall of separation and an "insensitive definition of the Establishment Clause." He accused the Court of establishing "a religion of secularism" by imposing artificial disadvantages upon traditional religion. He also held that the Court should not usurp decisions that should be left "for each local community and its school board."

Public opposition and congressional countermoves continued, especially on behalf of prayer. Some suggested that the prayers should be totally voluntary, perhaps even led by students rather than by teachers or administrators. Certainly the prayers should be "nondenominational," though presumably still recognizably Judeo-Christian. It was finally suggested that prayers be silent. By 1984 some 20 states had laws permitting a moment of silence each day in the public school classroom.

But then the Court invaded this sanctuary as well. In *Wallace* v. *Jaffree* (1985), a 6-to-3 majority found that a period of silence set aside for the purpose of prayer was still unconstitutional. It had no secular purpose, the Court ruled, and its primary effect was to advance religion. Because the state of Alabama specifically authorized a moment of silence "for meditation or voluntary prayer," that was its chief defect. As Justice Sandra Day O'Connor noted in a concurring opinion, purely voluntary prayer—before, during, or after school—has never been an issue before the Court. It was the governmental stipulation of prayer, even silent prayer, that created the problem, for "the conclusion is unavoidable that the purpose of the statute is to endorse prayer in the public school." However, O'Connor noted, a time of silence that did not have prayer as

Ishmael Jaffree challenged Alabama's law allowing a moment of silent prayer in schools. His objections were supported by the Supreme Court in 1985, though the dissents were unusually vigorous.

its stated purpose might pass all of the constitutional tests.

The dissents now were stronger, both in number and in tone. Chief Justice Warren Burger thought "the notion that the Alabama statute is a step toward creating an established church borders on, if it does not trespass into, the ridiculous." Justice Byron White called for "a basic reconsideration of our precedents" in the establishment clause cases. And Justice William Rehnquist, in a long and powerful dissent, dismissed not only many of the Court's precedents but also the prevailing understanding of constitutional and First Amendment history as well. He claimed that a proper understanding of the intentions of the framers "abundantly shows" that "nothing in the Establishment Clause requires government to be strictly neutral between religion and irreligion." Rehnquist added that, in view of George Washington's call for national prayer in the very year that the Bill of Rights was drawn up, "history must judge whether it was the father of his country in 1789, or a majority of the Court today, which has strayed from the meaning of the Establishment Clause."

The next case to be considered in this second category concerns baccalaureate services—religious ceremonies separate from the actual graduation formalities. These services have been standard fare in the nation's high schools (and often middle schools as well) for most if not all of the 20th century. In 1992 (*Lee* v. *Weisman*), the Court heard a case from Rhode Island that involved a 14-year-old girl graduating from a middle school and attending graduation exercises that included prayers to which she and her family objected.

The state, in its defense, explained that the student did not need to attend, if she had some conscientious objection to the prayers. But Justice Anthony Kennedy, for the Court's majority (a 5-to-4 decision), said that this was irrelevant—or worse. "Attendance may not be required by official decree, yet it is apparent that a student is not free to absent herself from the graduation exercise in any real sense of the term 'voluntary.'" Graduation, he noted, was a time for family celebration and recognition of a student's years of effort. "By any reading of our cases," Kennedy concluded, "the conformity required of the student in this case was too high an exaction to withstand the test of the Establishment Clause." Important and lengthy concurring opinions (Blackmun and Souter, joined by O'Connor and Stevens) supported Kennedy's conclusion.

Prayer and the U.S. Constitution

Among the many people who have proposed an amendment to the Constitution on behalf of prayer in the public schools was President Ronald Reagan, who submitted his proposal to Congress in 1982. Despite widespread support, both in Congress and among the public, and despite a highly visible Presidential push, Congress could not muster enough "ayes" for a two-thirds vote, as the Constitution requires. A good deal of the opposition stemmed from a reluctance to tamper with the First Amendment. The text of Reagan's proposed amendment follows.

Nothing in this Constitution shall be construed to prohibit individual or group prayer in public schools or other public institutions. No person shall be required by the United States or by any state to participate in prayer.

Deborah Weisman listens attentively to an address at her middle school commencement. Her father's request to ban prayers at the baccalaureate service was upheld by the Supreme Court.

But, as noted previously, the Court was sharply divided. Justice Antonin Scalia, in a dissent on behalf of himself and three others (Rehnquist, White, and Thomas) observed, "The history and tradition of our Nation are replete with public ceremonies featuring prayers of thanksgiving and petition." This being so, whatever the Court's majority said in *Lee,* invocations and benedictions would probably go on, "as they have for the past century and a half, so long as school authorities make clear that anyone who abstains from screaming in protest does not necessarily participate in the prayers." No one should be compelled to join in prayer, Scalia agreed, "but it is a shame to deprive our public culture of the opportunity, and indeed the encouragement, for people to do it voluntarily."

Finally on the matter of prayer and the public schools, in the year 2000 the Court heard a case from Texas concerning prayer and football games. School policy allowed a student, elected by a majority of classmates, to deliver a prayer over the public address system before all home football games. In *Santa Fe Independent School District* v. *Doe,* the Court by a vote of 6 to 3 found this practice to be unconstitutional. Writing for the majority, Justice John Paul Stevens observed that "it is beyond dispute that, at a minimum, the Constitution guarantees that government may not coerce anyone to support or participate in religion or its exercise, or otherwise act in a way which establishes a [state] religion or religious faith, or tends to do so." On the other hand, Chief Justice William Rehnquist, for the three dissenters, complained that the Court's opinion "bristles with hostility to all things religious in public life." He added that "nothing in the Establishment Clause prevents" the voters of this school district from making the choice that they did regarding prayer at their football games.

The cases considered above pertain not to instruction but to acts of religious worship within the public schools. Another category of cases concerns what is actually being taught as part of the regular academic program. In two widely watched Supreme Court cases, the curriculum in question was a scientific one: that is, what may be taught or must be taught regarding the origins of humankind. The convenient label applied to this issue is creationism versus Darwinism. Creationism relies on the Book of Genesis to explain the origins of all life in terms of direct divine action. Darwinism refers to the theories expounded by Charles Darwin during the 19th century, explaining the diversity of biological species in terms of evolution: that is, complex forms of life slowly developed, over millions of years, from simpler forms of life.

In 1968 the Court heard the first of the two cases, *Epperson* v. *Arkansas,* that concerned the teaching of biology in a high school in Little Rock, Arkansas. The state law in question harked back to the famous Scopes Trial in Dayton, Tennessee, in 1925. That case concerned a young biology instructor, John T. Scopes, who introduced the theory of evolution into his high school science classes. Such teaching, prohibited by state law at the time, led to the teacher's arrest and trial. Because Scopes was defended by the well-known criminal attorney Clarence Darrow and because former Presidential candidate William Jennings Bryan was assisting the prosecution, the case attracted national and even worldwide attention. With the relatively new technology of radio, audiences around the country listened eagerly to each day's developments or read full reports in the newspapers, none more biting than those Henry L. Mencken provided to the *Baltimore Sun.* Scopes, 25 years of age at the time of the trial, was found guilty and fined $100. The Tennessee State Supreme Court, however, overruled the Dayton court on merely technical grounds.

As a direct result of the Scopes case, Arkansas passed a law in 1928 making it unlawful in any state-supported institution "to teach the theory or doctrine that mankind ascended or descended from a lower order of animals" or to use any textbook that advocated such views. Justice Abe Fortas, speaking for the Court 40 years later in *Epperson* v. *Arkansas,* asserted that the State could not tailor its teaching and learning "to the principles or prohibitions of any religious sect or dogma. . . . In the present case, there can be no doubt that Arkansas has sought to prevent its teachers from discussing the theory of evolution because it is contrary to the belief of some that the Book of Genesis must be the exclusive source of doctrine as to the origin of man." The most remarkable aspect of this decision is that the vote was 9 to 0—a unanimous opinion in an area unaccustomed to such harmony of views.

Nearly 20 years later, the Court heard a somewhat similar case from Louisiana (*Edwards* v. *Aguillard,* 1987), and this time unanimity did not hold. The chief difference between the Louisiana and Arkansas cases was that Louisiana did not ban Darwinian theory but rather decreed that it had to be "balanced" by instruction in creationism. Justice William Brennan, speaking for the seven justices in the majority, found that the primary purpose of Louisiana's Creationism Act was "to advance a particular religious belief." Therefore, the law fell afoul of the establishment clause and its prohibitions. In a concurring opinion, Justice Lewis Powell, joined by Justice O'Connor, examined the legislative history of the Louisiana law and agreed with the lower courts that its language and thought were "not merely similar to the literal interpretation of Genesis; they are identical. . . ." However, both Powell and O'Connor reemphasized that "schoolchildren can and should be properly informed of all aspects of this Nation's religious heritage."

Justice Scalia, joined by Chief Justice Rehnquist, held that the Court had applied a much too rigid interpretation of the establishment clause in this instance, and in other cases "have made such a maze" of that clause "that even the most conscientious governmental officials can only guess what motives will be held unconstitutional." Moreover, they said, the Court dismissed too readily the secular purpose set forth in the act itself, calling into question the sincerity of the state legislators. The Court, Scalia added, responded almost with an automatic reflex, being seduced by "the facts and the legend" of the Scopes trial. "The people of Louisiana, including those who are Christian fundamentalists, are quite entitled, as a secular matter, to have whatever scientific evidence there may be against evolution presented in their schools, just as Mr. Scopes was entitled to present whatever evidence there was for it." And so there the case for or against Charles Darwin, for or against the Book of Genesis, somewhat uneasily rests.

The Scopes trial, dubbed the "monkey trial," received worldwide attention. John Scopes (second from left), in court with his lawyer Clarence Darrow (far left), taught evolution in his high school biology class.

These students attend a Bible reading group at their school. The Supreme Court in 1990 found such voluntary gatherings, not sponsored by the school, to be constitutional.

Under the canopy of what has sometimes been called a "Students' Bill of Rights," several groups have come to the defense of public school pupils in expressing their own religious opinions. For example, they argue that students should be allowed to distribute religious literature on campus, to do research papers on religious themes, to carry or study their Bibles on campus, and to be excused from classes where the content offends their religious views. In 1995 the Clinton administration also came to the defense of these and other rights, distributing guidelines to some 15,000 school superintendents that explained what degree of religious presence was permitted in the public schools. Secretary of Education Richard W. Riley indicated, "Schools may not discriminate against private religious expression by students, but must instead give students the same rights to engage in religious activity and discussion as they have to engage in other comparable activity." At the same time, however, "schools may not endorse religious activity or doctrine, nor may they coerce participation in religious activity." The Constitution, it was pointed out, does not require that public schools be "religion-free zones."

The U.S. Supreme Court weighed in on this issue in *Board of Education* v. *Mergens* (1990). Here the Court was asked to examine the constitutionality of the Equal Access Act, passed by the U.S. Congress, which permitted religious groups to meet on school grounds if other "noncurriculum related student groups" were allowed to do so. Groups such as stamp clubs and chess clubs, for example, did not relate to courses that the school offered; if groups like these were permitted, then religious groups could not be discriminated against. Justice O'Connor, writing for the majority, argued that this "equal access" did not amount to a governmental endorsement of religion. "We think that secondary school students are mature enough," she wrote, "and are likely to understand that a school does not endorse or support student speech that it merely permits on a nondiscriminatory basis." As a matter of free speech, O'Connor maintained, the school simply maintains a policy of "neutrality toward, rather than endorsement of, religious speech."

Though two justices partially dissented, they supported the majority conclusion. The only dissent, registered by Justice John Stevens, objected that the Court's interpretation opened public school doors far too wide. "Can Congress really have intended to issue an order to every public high school in the nation," Stevens asked, "stating, in substance, that if you sponsor a chess club, a scuba diving club, or a French club—without having formal classes in those subjects—you must also open your doors to every religious, political, or social organization no matter how controversial or distasteful its views may be?" He responded, "I think not."

In this case, the Court's majority took a welcome opportunity to say what was permitted in the public schools, rather than what was prohibited. And to many citizens, that moment had seemed a long time in coming. With all the attention given to religion in the public schools, one might conclude that the Supreme Court would have little to say about issues affecting private schools. However, this is far from true.

Chapter 6

The Establishment Clause: Private Schools

Government, especially state and local, has an obvious responsibility for the public, tax-supported schools but bears a less obvious responsibility for privately endowed schools. And yet the Supreme Court has been obliged to hear as many cases relating to private schools as to public schools. Regarding religion and the private schools, the legal problems primarily revolve around finances: that is, what sorts of monetary aids or subsidies government may provide.

In 1922 the State of Oregon passed a law requiring all mentally competent young people between the ages of 8 and 16 to attend the public schools. A military academy and a Catholic parochial school challenged the validity of this law, and by 1925 their suit had reached the Supreme Court. In *Pierce* v. *Society of Sisters,* a unanimous Court agreed that the Oregon law was in violation of the Fourteenth Amendment, for its effect would be to destroy all private or religious schools and thus to deprive the owners of their property "without due process of law." Justice James McReynolds, a Protestant, added that the Oregon law "unreasonably interferes with the liberty of parents and guardians to direct the upbringing and education of children under their control." Furthermore, "the child is not the mere creature of the state." This decision, often called the Magna Carta (the basic charter of liberty) of parochial schools, assured a place for private education in the United States from that time forward.

Parochial school students typically distinctive uniforms express their religious freedom in and out the classroom.

Like other religious groups before them, Muslims found it helpful to create their own private schools. These students at New Horizon School in Pasadena, California, wear distinctive uniforms and utilize special curriculum materials.

In that same decade the Louisiana legislature moved to assist the parochial schools by authorizing the purchase of secular textbooks for all of the state's children, whether in parochial or public schools. In 1930 the Supreme Court (*Cochran* v. *Louisiana State Board of Education*) weighed the constitutional merits of this law and found that it passed muster. Speaking for a unanimous Court, Chief Justice Charles Evans Hughes argued that the fiscal assistance was not to the religious school but to the pupil. "The school children and the state alone are the beneficiaries," he noted. This "child benefit" theory, as it came to be called, would be appealed to on subsequent occasions, in both state and federal courts.

The First Amendment did not play a part in either of these cases, but in 1947 the Court did apply the establishment clause to the states in *Everson* v. *Board of Education of Ewing Township.* Ewing Township, New Jersey, did not have its own fleet of school buses but compensated students who took public transportation to their respective schools, public or private. The issue, of course, was whether the state should reimburse bus fares to those students attending private (predominantly Roman Catholic) schools. Justice Hugo Black, speaking for the slim majority of five, harked back to the "child benefit" theory in stating that members of Catholic churches or of any other denomination could not "because of their faith, or lack of it" be excluded "from receiving the benefits of public welfare legislation." Providing public transportation to the parochial schools fell into the same category, Black argued, "as ordinary police and fire protection, connections for sewage disposal, public highways and sidewalks." "State power is no more to be used so as to handicap religions than it is to favor them." Then Black concluded with strong separationist language that left the four dissenters dumbfounded. "The First Amendment has erected a wall between church and state. That wall must be kept high and impregnable. We could not approve the slightest breach. New Jersey has not breached it here."

In a lengthy dissent, Justice Robert Jackson found the Court's language moving in one direction and its conclusion in a totally opposite one. It reminded him, he wryly observed, of a line from the English poet Lord Byron describing a young lady who, "whispering 'I will ne'er consent'—consented." Religious freedom was put first in the First Amendment, Jackson noted, "because it was first in the forefathers' minds; it was set forth in absolute terms, and its strength is in its rigidity." The amendment "was intended not only to keep the states' hands out of religion, but to keep religion's hands off the state." "Those great ends," he concluded, "I cannot but think are immeasurably compromised by today's decision."

In another lengthy opinion (in which all four dissenters joined), Justice Wiley Rutledge wrote that "two great drives" were constantly pushing to bring education and religion together in ways that the First Amendment forbids. "One is to introduce religious education and observances into the public schools. The other, to obtain public funds for the

The Necessity for Parochial Schools

Many denominations in America support and defend their own parochial schools. The largest of these systems, operated by the Roman Catholic Church, arose in the 19th century, in part as a reaction to the prevailing Protestantism evident in the public schools of that period. In 1884 the bishops issued a "pastoral letter" to the Catholic clergy, laying out the reasons for, indeed the necessity for, a comprehensive parochial school system. This is a portion of that letter.

The three great educational agencies are the home, the Church, and the school. These mold men and shape society. Therefore, each of them, to do its part well, must foster religion. But many, unfortunately, while avowing that religion should be the light and the atmosphere of the home and of the Church, are content to see it excluded from the school, and even advocate as the best school system that which necessarily excludes religion. Few surely will deny that childhood and youth are the periods of life when the character ought especially to be subjected to religious influences. Nor can we ignore the palpable fact that the school is an important factor in the forming of home and Church. It cannot, therefore, be desirable or advantageous that religion should be excluded from the school. On the contrary, it ought therefore to be one of the chief agencies for molding the young life to all that is true and virtuous, and holy. To shut religion out of the school, and keep it for home and the Church, is logically to train up a generation that will consider religion good for home and the Church, but not for the practical business of real life. But a more false and pernicious notion could not be imagined. Religion, in order to elevate a people, should inspire their whole life and rule their relations with one another. A life is not dwarfed, but ennobled by being lived in the presence of God. Therefore the school, which principally gives the knowledge fitting for practical life, ought to be under the holy influence of religion.

aid and support of various private religious schools." Both avenues, Rutledge added, "were closed by the Constitution. Neither should be opened by this Court." For good measure, Rutledge concluded by quoting James Madison and then appending, once again, the *Memorial and Remonstrance.*

The 5-to-4 decision in *Everson* was not easily arrived at, nor were the issues simple. And it is probably fair to say that after 1947 nothing will be simple again in cases regarding religion and the private schools. In an effort to clarify what is admittedly complex, the remaining cases will be considered under four categories: first, books and academic materials; second, salaries; third, tuition grants, vouchers, or tax credits; and fourth, church-related colleges.

In 1968 the Supreme Court decided a case from New York that concerned the free loan of textbooks to parochial schools. In *Board of Education* v. *Allen* a majority of the justices confirmed the 1930 Louisiana decision that approved such a loan, the "child benefit" concept being reaffirmed. Writing for the majority of six, Justice Byron White explained that the New York law "merely makes available to all school children the benefits of a general provision to lend school books free of charge." No aid went directly to the parochial school, only to the student. And, naturally, only secular books, approved by public school authorities, would be made available to the parochial schools.

In dissent, Justice Hugo Black declared that the New York law was "a flat, flagrant, open violation of the First and Fourteenth Amendments." He revealed his firm conviction that "tax-raised funds cannot constitutionally be used to support religious schools, buy their school books, erect their buildings, pay their teachers, or pay any other of their maintenance expenses, even to the extent of one penny." The only way to protect minority religious groups from majority groups, moreover, was "to keep the wall of separation between church and state high and impregnable." Justices William Douglas and Abe Fortas also wrote separate dissents, both arguing that the 1947 *Everson* case was not relevant here, for "there is nothing ideological about a bus." Textbooks, however, go "to the very heart of education in a parochial school."

Second graders in a parochial school in Connecticut learn about nature from their teacher, a Roman Catholic nun. Nuns taught secular as well as religious subjects.

The intricacies of this case pale before the complexities of *Meek* v. *Pittenger,* decided in 1975. The state of Pennsylvania had passed a convoluted law providing for the loan of textbooks to parochial schools and also for the loan of other instructional materials (including maps, photographs, musical scores, and recordings) along with audiovisual equipment and such "auxiliary services" as counseling, testing, psychological services, speech and hearing therapy, advanced classes, and remedial classes. The wide variety of services apparently required an equal number of distinctions by the Court. One justice, for example, "concurred in part and dissented in part" and filed a separate opinion in which one or two other justices joined—but only in part.

In the end, the Supreme Court voted 6 to 3 to void the Pennsylvania law, except for the loan of textbooks. All the other provisions, the Court held, would amount to "massive aid" to the parochial schools and would make it impossible "to separate secular educational functions from the predominantly religious role" performed by parochial schools. In addition, attempts to implement such a law would necessarily lead to both political and administrative "entanglement."

Chief Justice Warren Burger, in partial dissent, regretted that the majority had ruled out so much. "One can only hope," he said, "that, at some future date, the Court will come to a more enlightened and tolerant view" of the First Amendment's religion clauses. And Justice Rehnquist (joined by Justice White) indicated that he was "disturbed as much by the overtones of the Court's opinion as by its actual holding." Those overtones suggested that the Court should go beyond neutrality to "throw its weight on the side of those who believe that our society as a whole should be a purely secular one."

In this complex case of *Meek* v. *Pittenger,* some of the justices attempted to clarify the constitutional "tests" that the Court would apply to legislation. Three had already been specified in earlier cases: a law must have a secular purpose; the primary effect of the law must neither inhibit nor advance religion; and the law should not lead to "excessive government entanglement with religion." *Meek* added a fourth: the operation of the law in question should not result in political divisiveness along religious lines. Not all members of the Court were prepared to apply all four tests, but they did constitute something of a guideline—especially when nothing else seemed to help.

One other case deserves attention in this context: *Wolman* v. *Walter* (1977). The issue was an Ohio law that authorized funds to aid the parochial schools in purchasing secular textbooks; supplying standardized tests and scoring services; providing speech and hearing diagnostic services; offering therapy, guidance, and remedial service to certain students, though not on parochial school grounds; purchasing or lending instructional materials and instructional equipment that were "incapable of diversion to religious use"; and finally, financing field trips and services comparable to those found in the public schools.

Religious exercises are a regular part of the parochial school day. And there is nothing unconstitutional about such exercises— provided that no tax monies are involved.

The Court's opinion, rendered in eight separate sections, spoke to each of these provisions. Dissenters did the same, which made for something of a crazy-quilt pattern. The Court's summary stated: "we hold constitutional those portions of the Ohio statute authorizing the State to provide nonpublic school pupils with books, standardized testing and scoring, diagnostic services, and therapeutic and remedial services. We hold unconstitutional those portions relating to instructional materials and equipment and field trip services." It is no wonder that some justices complained in later cases that the line of separation "wavers" and that the Court is "groping for a rationale" (*PEARL* v. *Regan*, 1980).

A dozen years later, a case from Louisiana (*Mitchell* v. *Helms*) tested that wavering line once more and, in the opinion of many, made that line almost disappear. The question before the Supreme Court was this: whether public funds could be used to buy computers and other instructional materials for parochial schools. The Supreme Court had long approved the purchase of textbooks for secular subjects taught in the parochial schools. As Justice Sandra Day O'Connor noted in a concurring opinion, "Computers are now as necessary as were schoolbooks 30 years ago, and they play a somewhat similar role in the educational process." By a vote of 6 to 3, therefore, the Court found Louisiana's practice to be constitutional, overturning the ruling of a lower court.

Justice Clarence Thomas, writing for a plurality of four, found in the principles of neutrality and private choice all that was necessary to justify—on First Amendment grounds—this aid to parochial schools. Two justices, O'Connor and Breyer, joined in the expanded aid, but found the logic of Justice Thomas's opinion to be too sweeping. Three justices, led by David Souter, dissented, arguing that the establishment clause prohibited Congress or the state legislatures from passing any law "respecting an establishment of religion. It has been held to prohibit not only the institution of an official church, but any government act favoring religion, a particular religion, or for that matter irreligion. Thus it bars the use of public funds for religious aid." Some observers saw in the majority opinion a harbinger of even more direct aid to private schools in the form of vouchers. They were right.

On the matter of salaries, the Supreme Court in 1971 heard two cases together, one originating in Pennsylvania (*Lemon* v. *Kurtzman*) and the other in Rhode Island (*Earley* v. *DiCenso*). The Rhode Island case dealt with a 1969 law providing a state supplement of 15 percent to be paid to teachers in nonpublic schools. In Pennsylvania, a 1968 law authorized direct reimbursement of teachers' salaries in nonpublic schools, carefully limited to courses "presented in the curricula of the public schools." Both state laws were responding to a fiscal crisis in the private and parochial schools.

The salary subsidies doomed these state laws, and they did so with a certitude not often seen in this area. Only Justice Byron White registered a partial dissent. Chief Justice Warren Burger, writing on behalf of the Court, reviewed the operation of the laws in their respective states. In Rhode Island, some 25 percent of the state's pupils attended nonpublic

The question of religious symbolism in the parochial school classroom presented difficulties for the Supreme Court in 1971 as it evaluated salary subsidies for parochial school teachers.

schools; of these, 95 percent were in schools affiliated with the Roman Catholic Church. And the 250 teachers who had taken advantage of the state's 15 percent subsidy were all employed by Roman Catholic schools. In Pennsylvania, more than 20 percent of the students attended nonpublic schools. "More than 96% of these pupils attend church-related schools, and most of these schools are affiliated with the Roman Catholic Church," Burger indicated. Though the term *nonpublic* covers private schools of all kinds, in these two states most students attending private schools were enrolled in Roman Catholic parochial schools.

Burger conceded that the legislative intent was a secular one: namely, "to enhance the quality of secular education in all schools covered by the compulsory attendance laws." In this respect the states' laws did not offend the religion clauses of the First Amendment. Nonetheless, the Court found that, because of the obvious religious character of the schools, those laws led to "excessive entanglement between government and religion." In Rhode Island, for example, "the school buildings contain identifying religious symbols such as crosses on the exterior and crucifixes, and religious paintings and statues either in the classrooms or hallways." Moreover, about "two-thirds of the teachers in these schools are nuns of various religious orders." Their presence accentuated the religious character and purpose of these schools.

And that "substantial religious character" created the "entangling church-state relationships of the kind the Religion Clauses sought to avoid." We do not charge any of these parochial school teachers with bad faith, Burger said, in trying to keep separate the religious and secular purposes in their instructional program. "We simply recognize that a dedicated religious person, teaching in a school affiliated with his or her faith and operated to inculcate its tenets, will inevitably experience great difficulty in remaining religiously neutral." He asserted that the state would experience great difficulty, as well, in trying to ensure that the several legal restrictions were properly and carefully enforced. In fact, this would require a "comprehensive, discriminating, and continuing state surveillance." And this would surely lead to that "excessive entanglement" that the Court wished to avoid.

In 1993 the Court heard an additional case (*Zobrest* v. *Catalina School District*) that involved salaries, but with major differences from the Pennsylvania and Rhode Island cases discussed above. Only a single salary was at issue: that of an interpreter for a deaf student attending a Roman Catholic high school in Arizona. Also, this suit rested in part on a Disabilities Education Act that required the state of Arizona to distribute federal funds to children identified as "handicapped."

James Zobrest attended a school for the deaf for grades one through five. He then attended a public school for grades six through eight, and the state provided an interpreter for him. For religious reasons, James's parents transferred him to Salpointe Catholic High School for his ninth grade. When the state, on First Amendment grounds, declined to cover the salary of an interpreter in this sectarian school, the parents sued to recover the more than $7,000 in salary they had been obliged to pay.

Chief Justice William Rehnquist, on behalf of the majority of five justices, found in favor of the Zobrest family. No salary funds, he pointed out, ever went to the sectarian school. Nor was this high school "relieved of an expense that it otherwise would have assumed in educating its students." The Disabilities Education Act did provide some money for James's education, but "handicapped children, not sectarian schools, are the primary beneficiaries," Rehnquist pointed out. He concluded that the presence of a sign-language interpreter neither added to nor subtracted from the religious environment of the school, and therefore the establishment clause prohibitions did not apply.

Four dissenters argued that the case should have been settled, not on a constitutional issue but in terms of Arizona's own statutes and regulations. Two of the four, however, dissented also on grounds of substance as well as procedure. Justice Harry Blackmun (joined by Justice David Souter) stated, "Until now, the Court never authorized a public employee to participate directly in religious indoctrination." The interpreter did not function like some inanimate tape recorder but would be interpreting at the daily Masses as well as in religion classes and all references to the divine. Thus, "the

James Zobrest talks with his parents after learning that the Supreme Court ruled in his favor. He had been denied a state-paid sign language interpreter while attending a parochial high school.

interpreter's every gesture would be infused with religious significance." Blackmun concluded that the Court was straying "from the course set by nearly five decades of Establishment Clause jurisprudence. Accordingly, I dissent." (A somewhat similar case, though it did not involve salaries, came to the Supreme Court in 1986 from the state of Washington. The question involved the claim of a blind student, Larry Witters, to rehabilitation funds even though he attended a private Christian college to prepare himself for the ministry. Without dissent, the Court found in his favor.)

The issue of tuition grants or vouchers, as well as tax credits for students attending private schools, has been a lively one in citizen discussion groups since the 1970s, and the Court first considered it in *PEARL* v. *Nyquist* (1973). A New York law that took effect in 1972 offered tuition compensation to parents whose children attended elementary or secondary nonpublic schools. To qualify, parents had to have an annual taxable income of less than $5,000. The payment amounted to $50 apiece for elementary school students and $100 apiece for secondary school students. In no case could the reimbursement exceed 50 percent of the tuition. In addition, the law placed no restrictions on how the parents could use the grants. (Of New York's 2,038 nonpublic schools, 1,415 were Catholic, 164 Jewish, 59 Lutheran, 49 Episcopal, 37 Seventh-day Adventist, and 18 affiliated with other religious groups. Approximately 85 percent of all the private schools in New York were, therefore, religiously affiliated.)

The Court, with Justice Lewis Powell as spokesman, reviewed the state's arguments for such payments. First, they would help to maintain a vital and pluralistic society; second, they would give lower-income families an option for alternative education that they did not previously possess; and third, they would prevent a swift decline in nonpublic schools, an occurrence that would only serve to intensify the fiscal crisis faced by public education. Yet these substantial reasons, Powell wrote, "must be weighed against the relevant provisions and purposes of the First Amendment, which safeguard the separation of Church from State and have been regarded from the beginning as among the most cherished features of our constitutional system." Viewed in this light, the New York law (along with a second New York law and one from Pennsylvania, which were being reviewed at the same time) failed to pass the test. The majority concluded that their primary effect was to advance religion.

Three justices (Burger, White, and Rehnquist) dissented from parts of the majority decision, but only Justice Byron White disagreed with all of it. Chief Justice Burger specifically defended the New York and Pennsylvania tuition grant programs. While admitting that the Court's decisions regarding the religion clauses ran in "no straight line," Burger said that at least one "solid, basic principle" had been laid down: namely, "that the Establishment Clause does not forbid governments, state or federal, from enacting a program of general welfare under which benefits are distributed to private individuals." Justice White also saw the state laws as merely assisting nonpublic schools in carrying out their secular function. This was the "overriding consequence of these laws and the resulting, but incidental, benefit to religion should not invalidate them."

Ten years later, the Court heard a similar case from Minnesota, *Mueller* v. *Allen.* This time the majority upheld the tax credits granted to parents whose children were in either private or public schools. (In the school year prior to the Court's decision, more than 800,000 Minnesota children attended public schools; about 90,000 were in private schools. Of those 500 private schools, some 95 percent had a religious affiliation.) Minnesota's laws permitted state taxpayers to deduct from their reported gross income up to $500 per child in the first six grades and up to $700 per child in grades seven through twelve. These deductions, available to all parents of all schoolchildren, were limited to actual expenses that parents incurred for tuition, textbooks, and transportation.

Chief Justice Rehnquist, writing for the majority of five, held that the Minnesota law met all of the Court's tests for determining whether the First Amendment had been violated. First, Minnesota's plan had a secular purpose: it helped parents defray the costs of educating their children. Second, it did not have the primary effect "of advancing the sectarian aims of the nonpublic school." This, said the majority, is because no monies go directly to the school, only to the parents by way of a tax credit. Third, no excessive entanglement was involved because the kind of "comprehensive, discriminating,, and continuing state surveillance" disal-

lowed in the 1973 cases was not required here. In view of all this, the Court's majority found the Minnesota arrangement to be constitutional.

Justice Thurgood Marshall wrote the dissenting opinion, in which three other justices joined. Though the tax credits were available to all parents, Marshall pointed out, in actual practice the chief benefit went to those parents whose children attended the parochial schools. "Parents who send their children to free public schools," he wrote, "are simply ineligible to obtain the full benefit of the deduction except in the unlikely event that they buy $700 worth of pencils, notebooks, and bus rides for their school-age children." So far as the First Amendment was concerned, Marshall added, a tax credit did not differ from a direct grant to parents, and that had already been found unconstitutional. The majority saw

The controversy surrounding public funding for parochial schools extends to institutions of higher education as well. Brigham Young University (Mormon), however, has not accepted federal funding and is therefore removed from the debate.

121

In Cleveland, Ohio, Roberta Kitchen assists her eleven-year-old daughter, Toshika, in preparing her math homework for a parochial school that she entered under the voucher program approved in 2002.

significant differences between the 1983 Minnesota case and *PEARL* v. *Nyquist*. Marshall and his fellow dissenters did not.

The significance of these cases lies in the continued effort to broaden government support for nonpublic schools. "Voucher plans" of many kinds have been proposed by several states, under which parents receive a voucher for a specified amount of money that may be used for their child's education in either private or public school. Most of these programs have been modest and experimental in nature. In 1995, for example, the governor of Ohio urged that $5 million be set aside for a pilot project confined to the city of Cleveland. The legislature approved the plan and in the school year 1996–97 the program got underway.

Opponents of this pilot program promised to carry their protest all the way to the Supreme Court, which they did. And in a 5 to 4 decision handed down in 2002 *(Zelman* v. *Simmons-Harris)*, they lost. By the terms of Ohio's law, vouchers worth up to $2,250 may be issued to parents, who can then decide where they will apply these vouchers. Thus far, only private schools have participated in this program, and 82 percent of these schools are religious. All private schools agree not to discriminate in their admissions on the basis of race, religion, or ethnic background. Writing for the majority, Chief Justice William Rehnquist summarized the case as follows: ". . . the Ohio program is entirely neutral with respect to religion. It provides benefits directly to a wide spectrum of individuals, defined only by financial need and residence in a particular school district. It permits such individuals to exercise genuine choice among options public and private, secular and religious. The program is therefore a program of true private choice."

On behalf of the four dissenters, Justice David Souter argued that the decision of the majority violated precedent set by the Court going all the way back to 1947 (*Everson* v. *Board of Education of Ewing Township*). There the Court asserted that "No tax in any amount, large or small, can be levied to support any religious activities or institutions, whatever they may be called, or whatever form they may adopt to teach or practice religion." Souter and his fellow dissenters believed that the decision in *Zelman* violated both the letter and the spirit of that long-standing precedent. The voucher money, Souter wrote, will "pay for eligible students' instruction not only in secular subjects but in religion as well, in schools that can be fairly characterized as founded to teach religious doctrine and to imbue teaching in all subjects with a religious dimension."

But if the Court pointed in one direction in Ohio, the public pointed in another in referenda in Colorado, California, Oregon, and Washington, where voucher programs were decisively defeated. So the Ohio decision may not lead to a wholesale adoption of voucher usage, as the supporters of that decision hope, and as the opponents fear. Some observers even argue that the Cleveland case is unique since the state was obliged in 1995 to take over a failing public school system. American society will no doubt continue to be troubled by issues pertaining to public and parochial schools, especially as these issues impinge upon the religion clauses of the First Amendment.

On the level of church-related higher education, there is generally less passion than in the cases considered above. In 1971, 1973, and 1976 the

Supreme Court heard cases concerning the disbursement of government funds to sectarian institutions of higher education. As a rule, a majority of justices worried less about religious indoctrination and exposure to religious symbols when the students were of college age than when they were in elementary or secondary schools. Not only were the college students more mature, but the compulsory attendance laws did not apply to them. The dissenting minority, on the other hand, saw little constitutional difference between federal aid for a church-related college and federal aid for a church-related school. And the colleges, for their part, seemed much less certain that their "sectarian" nature infiltrated the entire institution in the way that it presumably did in most parochial schools. Keeping these broad observations in mind, the three cases can be briefly summarized.

In *Tilton* v. *Richardson* (1971), the question was whether federal money (under the Higher Education Facilities Act) could be used to erect buildings on four Catholic college campuses in Connecticut. The buildings were secular in nature: two libraries, a fine arts facility, a science structure, and a language laboratory. In a 5-to-4 decision, the Court majority declared, "There is no evidence that religion seeps into the use of any of these facilities." Moreover, the aid here consisted of a "one-time, single purpose construction grant." The dissenters argued that whether federal money was given once or many times was beside the point. A single violation of the establishment clause was as unconstitutional as repeated violations.

A case heard two years later, *Hunt* v. *McNair,* concerned a Baptist college in Charleston, South Carolina, and its ability to utilize the state's financing plan to borrow money at a lower rate than would otherwise be possible. The 6-to-3 majority found no violation of the First Amendment here, because the borrowed money would not be used for any building given over to sectarian instruction or worship. The dissenters held that South Carolina would indeed be aiding a religious institution, "while the College, in turn, surrenders to the State a comprehensive and continuing surveillance of the educational, religious, and fiscal affairs of the College."

Finally, a 1976 Maryland case (*Roemer* v. *Board of Public Works*) resulted in another narrow 5-to-4 decision. A Maryland law provided an annual subsidy to any private institution of higher learning, except those that awarded "only seminarian or theological degrees." The majority saw no constitutional prohibition, one justice commenting that the "excessive entanglement" test appeared no less "curious and mystifying" than when it was first introduced. The dissenters repeated a now familiar refrain: "The discrete interests of government and religion are mutually best served when each avoids too close a proximity to the other."

Clearly, the Court had moved a long way from the unanimous and brief decisions rendered in 1925 in Oregon and in 1930 in Louisiana. That move was certainly toward complexity—away from simplicity and perhaps even clarity. In the Maryland case just discussed, the Court's majority, after reviewing most of the suits covered in this chapter, admitted that "the slate we write on is anything but clean." Perhaps this is but another of those instances where U.S. society must look beyond the Supreme Court to solve many of its political, educational, or moral dilemmas.

Chapter 7

The Free-Exercise Clause: Religious Liberty

The establishment clause of the First Amendment indicates that government may not assist or advance religion. The free-exercise clause, by contrast, states that the government may not penalize or inhibit religion. They are two sides of the same coin, designed to ensure neutrality on the part of government and maximum freedom for individual citizens to choose their form of religious worship, or choose not to worship at all. Those most in danger of having their "free exercise" cramped or denied tend to be members of minority (that is, nonmainstream) religious groups. For this reason, the major Supreme Court cases dealing with the free-exercise clause can be conveniently grouped according to the minority denominations that were parties to the legal action.

In the 20th century, the appropriate place to begin, both chronologically and in terms of the number of suits, is with the Jehovah's Witnesses. This religious body, founded in 1872, is best known for its vigorous evangelizing activity (both in the United States and abroad), an activity that most Americans are familiar with through door-to-door solicitation, usually accompanied by the sale or distribution of literature. Those techniques are responsible for many of the cases that reached the Supreme Court, though not for all of them. Widely persecuted both in the United States and abroad, especially in wartime (for the Witnesses decline to bear arms), the group continues to grow, with world membership now exceeding 4 million.

erican Sikhs stage a test at the United tions in 1984. Sikhs wear bans in accordance with ir religious beliefs, and st state laws guarantee wearer this right without suffering any penalty discrimination.

127

These children read *The Watchtower,* a publication of the Jehovah's Witnesses, during their suspension from school for refusing to salute the American flag.

In *Cantwell* v. *Connecticut* (1940), the Supreme Court for the first time explicitly applied the free-exercise clause of the First Amendment to the states. Earlier cases involving the Jehovah's Witnesses had been decided on the grounds of free speech or free press. But now in 1940 the Court turned its attention directly to the free exercise of religion. Not since the Mormon cases of 1879 and 1890 had the Court concentrated so closely on the precise meaning of free exercise for a religious minority.

Jehovah's Witness Newton Cantwell and his two sons, Jesse and Russell, played records on a portable phonograph in a crowded New Haven neighborhood inhabited chiefly by Roman Catholics. The records, clearly anti-Catholic in both tone and substance, led to the Cantwells' being charged with disturbing the peace and violating a state law that regulated the conditions under which solicitation of money or subscriptions could be made. The Witnesses had not applied for an official permit before proceeding to sell their literature or accept contributions. Violations were punishable by fines of up to $100 or a maximum jail term of 30 days, or both.

For the Court, Justice Owen Roberts acknowledged that religious propaganda could sometimes be disturbing, even offensive. But the people of the United States, he added, "have determined that in spite of the probability of excesses and abuses, [the free exercise of religion is] essential to enlightened opinion and right conduct on the part of the citizens of a democracy." This was especially evident, Roberts noted, if one took "the long view." Government could not interfere with free exercise unless it found "a clear and present danger to a substantial interest of the State." Apart from such a finding, "a state may not unduly suppress free communication of ideas, religious or otherwise, under the guise of conserving desirable conditions." The opinion was brief, and the justices were unanimous.

Those circumstances quickly changed. In a 1942 case (*Jones* v. *Opelika*) the judgment was 5 to 4 against the Witnesses, and in a 1943 case (*Murdock* v. *Commonwealth of Pennsylvania*) the judgment was 5 to 4 in their favor. Both of these cases involved the sale and distribution of religious literature and were therefore similar to the 1940 *Cantwell* case. The difference lay chiefly in the Court itself, as the justices saw the free-exercise issue as more complicated than it had at first appeared to be.

From a unanimous opinion in 1940, to two 5 to 4 decisions in the early 1940s, the Court a half-century later moved back toward unanimity. In the *Watchtower Bible & Tract Society* v. *Village of Stratton* [Ohio], the Court in 2002 agreed by a vote of 8 to 1 that Jehovah's Witnesses did not need a permit from the mayor's office to carry on their door-to-door ministry. "It is offensive . . . to the very notion of a free society," Justice John Paul Stevens wrote for the majority, "that in the context of everyday public discourse a citizen must first inform the government of her desire

The U.S. Supreme Court in 2002 ruled that a municipal requirement that all persons making door-to-door calls must have a permit was unconstitutional. Mayor John Abdalla, who supported the requirement, stands behind his bar in the town in question: Stratton, Ohio.

to speak to her neighbors, and then obtain a permit to do so." The sole dissenter, Chief Justice William Rehnquist, thought the necessity to secure a permit was a useful measure for crime control. "The Constitution does not require," he wrote, "that Stratton first endure its own crime wave before it takes measures to prevent crime." If the village ordinance had been applied only to commercial activities and the solicitation of funds, it might well have been found constitutional. But once again the free exercise of religion occupied a privileged position in constitutional jurisprudence.

The best-known Jehovah's Witness cases had nothing to do with proselytizing activities; rather, they concerned the saluting of the American flag in the public schools. In *Minersville School District* v. *Gobitis* (1940), the Court considered the expulsion of Lillian Gobitas (age 12) and her brother William (age 10) from their Pennsylvania school for refusing, on religious grounds, to salute the American flag. (The Supreme Court case is officially *Minersville School District* v. *Gobitis*. The actual spelling of the name is *Gobitas*. So the inconsistency is built in and unavoidable.)

"The children," the Court noted, "had been brought up conscientiously to believe that such a gesture of respect for the flag was forbidden by command of scripture." So here the Court had to balance a sincere religious claim against the claim of national interest. "Our present task then," Justice Felix Frankfurter wrote for the majority of eight, "as so often is the case with courts, is to reconcile two rights in order to prevent either from destroying the other. But, because in safeguarding conscience we are dealing with interests so subtle and so dear, every possible leeway should be given to the claims of religious faith."

Anyone reading that last sentence might well be excused for thinking that Frankfurter and his majority would come down solidly on the side of Lillian and William Gobitas. But that did not happen. Rather, Frankfurter argued with eloquence and at some length that national interest and national unity required the enforcement of the flag salute. "The ultimate foundation of a free society," he wrote, "is the binding tie of cohesive sentiment. . . .

William and Lillian Gobitas, standing on either side of their father, testified in court that saluting the flag violated their religious principles. They quoted biblical passages to bolster their testimony.

[The] flag is the symbol of our national unity, transcending all internal differences, however large, within the framework of the Constitution."

In registering the single dissent, Justice Harlan Stone admitted that the constitutional guarantees of personal liberties were not, could not be, "absolutes." "But it is a long step, and one which I am unable to take, to the positions that government [may] compel public affirmations" that violate the religious consciences of the young. If those personal liberties have any meaning at all, Stone affirmed, they must at a minimum guarantee the "freedom of the individual from compulsion as to what he shall think and what he shall say, at least where the compulsion is to bear false witness to his religion." Voluntary expressions of loyalty might well promote national unity, in Stone's view, but compulsory expressions by children, especially when they violate their own and their parents' religious convictions, were quite another matter.

The force of Stone's dissent stuck in the minds of several justices as they heard strong public criticism from both legal scholars and religious leaders. Some justices were also distressed to learn that elements of the public interpreted the Court's decision to mean that brutal persecution of the Witnesses had federal approval. In addition, the composition of the Court changed, as two newly appointed justices—Robert Jackson and Wiley Rutledge—arrived in 1941 and 1943, respectively. Nonetheless, the dramatic reversal (again by an 8-to-1 vote) that emerged in *West Virginia State Board of Education* v. *Barnette* came as a surprise to many—especially since the nation was in the midst of World War II—and as a blow to some, none more than Felix Frankfurter.

Justice Jackson, one of the new appointees, wrote on behalf of the eight-man majority. Relying more on freedom of speech and of the press than of religion, Jackson agreed with Stone that national unity by persuasion did not deserve to be mentioned in the same breath with national unity by compulsion. "If there is any fixed star in our constitutional constellation," Jackson pronounced, "it is that no official, high or petty, can prescribe what shall be orthodox in politics, nationalism, religion, or other matters of opinion, or force citizens to confess by word or act their faith therein." He concluded: "If there are any circumstances which per-

mit an exception, they do not now occur to us." Back in the Minersville School District of Pennsylvania, Lillian and William Gobitas could now return to their public school, and they would no longer be required, in violation of their religious consciences, to salute the flag.

A second category of cases concerned Jewish Orthodoxy and Seventh-day Adventism. Because the states and communities of America bubble over with Sunday laws and Sunday regulations, the Supreme Court has had many opportunities to hear suits against these laws. Not until 1961, however, did the Court accept such cases, and then it accepted four of them at once: one from Maryland, two from Pennsylvania, and one from New York. In two instances, the plaintiffs charged that the establishment clause was being violated, and in the other two the complaint concerned the free-exercise clause.

In *Braunfeld* v. *Brown* and in *Gallagher* v. *Crown Kosher Super Market,* Orthodox Jewish businessmen complained that the Sunday laws

Sunday closing laws caused economic hardships for Jewish shop owners and businessmen because they refused to work on their Sabbath, Saturday. As a result, their stores remained closed for the entire weekend.

(of New York and Pennsylvania) imposed a serious economic hardship on them, for their own religion compelled them to be closed on Saturday (the Jewish Sabbath) and the state then compelled them to be closed on Sunday. For this reason, they were subject to unfair competition from businesses that had to close only one day a week. Both Abraham Braunfeld of Philadelphia, a seller of clothing and home furnishings, and the Crown Kosher Super Market of New York claimed that the resulting burden on a free exercise of their religion violated the First Amendment.

Chief Justice Earl Warren wrote the majority opinion in all four Sunday laws cases. While conceding that the observance of Sunday had started out as a religious (Christian) holy day, Warren explained that it had now become a secular holiday. Its religious origins were no longer relevant, he added, for it "is common knowledge that the first day of the week has come to have special significance as a rest day in this country." People of all religions or none, the Court majority observed, regarded Sunday as a time for family activity of one sort or another. And surely the state had a right, on health and welfare grounds, to set aside one day in seven as a day of rest and relaxation. If this worked an economic hardship on some because of their religious convictions, this would only be "an indirect burden" on the free exercise of religion. The Court, therefore, by a margin of 6 to 3, upheld all four Sunday laws.

Justice Douglas was equally sweeping: he rejected all four laws as unconstitutional. "The question," he wrote, was "not whether one day out of seven can be imposed by a State as a day of rest." On the contrary, the question was "whether a State can impose criminal sanctions on those who, unlike the Christian majority that makes up our society, worship on a different day or do not share the religious scruples of the majority." Dissenting only to the two free-exercise cases, Justices William Brennan and Potter Stewart saw administrative convenience (the same day of "rest" for all) taking precedence over a religious liberty. Stewart put the matter succinctly: "A law which compels an Orthodox Jew to choose between his religious faith and his economic survival . . . is a cruel choice." He added that in his view such a choice "no State can constitutionally demand."

Nevertheless, Orthodox Jews and others seemed stuck with that choice—at least for a time. In 1963 the Court heard a case involving a Seventh-day Adventist who was fired by her South Carolina employer because she declined to work on Saturday—her Sabbath. When Adell Sherbert applied for unemployment benefits, these were denied because she would not accept "suitable employment" if it involved working on Saturdays. Justice Brennan, who dissented in the two Sunday-closing cases noted above, now wrote the majority opinion for the Court. It is not surprising, then, that he found South Carolina guilty of imposing an undue burden on Sherbert's free exercise of religion. The ruling, he explained, did not in any way amount to an "establishment of Seventh-day Adventist religion in South Carolina." The Court only required that government be neutral in the face of religious differences.

The Supreme Court ruled that Adell Sherbert, a Seventh-day Adventist, could not be denied unemployment benefits because she refused to work on her Saturday Sabbath.

This case did produce some surprises, however. First, the Court backed Brennan's opinion by a vote of 7 to 2, an amazing turnaround because just two years earlier the Court had voted 6 to 3 on the opposite side. Second, this case extended the free-exercise protections further than any previous Court decision had done. And the final surprise is that the Adventist case did not lead to a rehearing or reversal of the two 1961 cases involving Orthodox Jews—mainly because the states in question quietly amended their laws to allow Sabbatarians to be excused from the general Sunday requirements. Earlier, the Court had declared such exemptions unjustified. But after *Sherbert* v. *Verner,* this position no longer made any sense.

A third category of cases involved the Amish. Dating back to the days of the Protestant Reformation in the 16th century, the Amish never quite "joined" any larger society. Like Anabaptists, Mennonites, and others often called the Radical Reformers, the Amish encountered persecution from Lutherans, Calvinists, and Catholics alike. They believed in separation of church and state—a most unusual and intolerable idea in 16th-century Europe; they tried to maintain their traditional way of life against all intrusions of the modern world; and they offended many governments by their steady embrace of pacifism. As early as 1730 Amish settlers came to North America, initially to Pennsylvania, but later to Ohio, Indiana, and Wisconsin. The Amish were mainly farmers, but their agricultural life and their religious life so overlapped that any separation between them was difficult. Holding strictly to the patterns of

Amish men gather at the Internal Revenue Service to protest their need to contribute to social security. Because the Amish had separated themselves from larger society, they argued that they should be exempt from following certain federal regulations, such as compulsory education and federal tax laws.

their German and Swiss forebears, the Amish rejected the use of automobiles and electricity and refused to marry outside the community. What these "peculiar people" desired most was to be left alone, but that proved difficult, especially when they ran up against compulsory education laws in state after state.

In 1950, 13 Amish bishops drew up a statement explaining why they opposed having their children in the public schools beyond the eighth grade. After that grade, Amish boys and girls would continue to receive education, but this would take place on the farm or in the household—and under the direct supervision of the parents. Furthermore, the bishops added, "our children should be well and properly taught in the Scriptures" in the German language, and no public schools provided this sort of education. Moreover, if Amish adolescents mixed with young people of other beliefs and lifestyles, this would likely lead to marriages outside the community. That, the bishops believed, would directly threaten the Amish way of life and possibly even lead to its extinction. Finally, the bishops declared that requiring their children to stay in school beyond the eighth grade constituted "an interference with the religious rights and liberties which were promised to our forefathers when they came to America, and which are granted to us by the Constitution of our State [Pennsylvania] and our Nation."

For some years the Amish tried to maintain their own "vocational high schools," but these rarely met state standards in curriculum or in matters of health and safety. So the Amish, often fined and jailed, engaged in frequent confrontations with state education officials. When taken to court, they regularly lost. All that ended in 1972, when the U. S. Supreme Court ruled unanimously in their favor in *Wisconsin* v. *Yoder*.

Amish students Frieda Yoder (age 15), Barbara Miller (15), and Vernon Yetzy (14) had all finished the eighth grade in the public schools of Greene County, Wisconsin. Their parents, members of the most conservative branch of the movement, the Old Order Amish, declined to keep them in the public schools until they were 16 years old, as Wisconsin law required. And the parents based this refusal on their constitutional right to the free exercise of their religion.

Chief Justice Warren Burger acknowledged that the Old Order Amish believed "that salvation requires life in a church community separate and apart from the world and worldly influence." He also acknowledged that the state had a substantial interest in universal education for all its citizens. But the state's right, he argued, "is not totally free from a balancing process when it impinges on other fundamental rights," especially those guaranteed by the First Amendment. And the Chief Justice was much impressed that the Amish, for hundreds of years, had managed to be responsible citizens who were in no way a charge upon public welfare or a threat to the peace and stability of society. In the historical record, Burger noted, there was "strong evidence that they are capable of fulfilling the social and political responsibilities of citizenship without compelled attendance beyond the eighth grade." Further, such compulsion made even less sense when it came at "the price of jeopardizing their free exercise of religious belief."

In ruling in the Amish's favor, Burger wished to make it clear that this did not open the floodgates to others who might wish to escape the force of the compulsory attendance laws. "It cannot be over-emphasized," he wrote, "that we are not dealing with a way of life and mode of education by a group claiming to have recently discovered some 'progressive' or more enlightened process for rearing children in modern life." And Justice William Douglas, in a partial dissent, also wanted the wishes of the Amish children to be as carefully explored as those of the parents. In any event, the Court here clearly carved out a special niche in the law for this small (the Old Order Amish number about 20,000), dedicated, hardworking, sincere religious group.

Two decades later, in 1994, the Supreme Court heard a case involving a strict sect within Hasidic Judaism: *Board of Education of Kiryas Joel Village School District* v. *Louis Grunet et al.* Although this case was decided more on the grounds of the establishment clause of the First Amendment rather than the free-exercise clause, it nonetheless offers an interesting comparison as the Court tries to determine the limits of accommodation to a minority religion. The Kiryas Joel Village, a small community of some 12,000 residents about 50 miles northwest of New York City,

sought public funding for the education of 200 to 300 handicapped and learning-disabled children. The legislature of New York responded with a law that carved out a special school district for these Hasidic Jewish children. By a vote of 6 to 3, the Court's majority found that political boundaries had been drawn on religious, rather than on neutral, grounds. And that, said Justice David Souter for the majority, is an establishment of religion, not merely an accommodation. For the three dissenters, Justice Antonin Scalia vigorously disagreed, asserting that "once this Court has abandoned text and history as guides, nothing prevents it from calling religious toleration the establishment of religion."

The New York State Legislature, having found its law declared unconstitutional, went back to the drawing board and drew up a new law that

Hasidic Jews picket in front of the Supreme Court during arguments in the Kiryas Joel School District case. This case posed the delicate question: when does accommodation of religion become governmental support of religion?

A Santeria devotee and her child sit in the Iglesia Lukumi Babalu Aye, the first Santerian church in Florida. The objects on the left are religious items used in church services.

the State Supreme Court of New York upheld in 1995. The New York State Court of Appeals, however, in 1997 found this new law unconstitutional as well. Beyond that, all did not proceed smoothly within the Hasidic village of Kiryas Joel itself. Dissidents in the small sect argued that the school district was being run like a theocracy and that it even tried to dictate the choice of a grand rabbi. In 1997 the village settled a $300,000 lawsuit filed by the dissident members. The deputy mayor of the village commented: "I feel this is a victory for everyone because the primary purpose in life is that people should be able to live together." In all of the Supreme Court's deliberations and dissents, that simple principle can easily drop from view.

Of all the minority religions raising issues before the Supreme Court, the least known may well be Santeria (literally, "the way of the saints"), which emerged from the beliefs of African slaves who arrived in Cuba by the hundreds of thousands in the 19th century and before. Elements of African religion (specifically that of the Yoruba people of present-day Nigeria) mixed with elements of Roman Catholicism to create Santeria. After the rise of the Castro regime in Cuba during the late 1950s, many adherents of Santeria sought greater religious freedom by fleeing to Florida, with large numbers settling in the town of Hialeah. In the 1990s Santeria membership in South Florida was estimated to be between 50,000 and 60,000.

The ritual practice of animal sacrifice led this group into conflict with city authorities and brought their case ultimately to the Supreme Court (*Church of the Lukumi Babalu Aye* v. *City of Hialeah,* 1993). Church members sacrificed many kinds of animals (chickens, pigeons, doves, ducks, goats, sheep, and turtles) on the occasion of births, marriages, and deaths; to cure the sick; to initiate new members and priests; and during their annual celebration. Although animal sacrifice has a long tradition in African, Middle Eastern, and other religions, it struck many U.S. citizens in the 20th century as odd or offensive—perhaps even illegal. As early as 1987, the city council of Hialeah began passing a series of ordinances designed to prevent "the possibility of public ritualistic animal sacrifice." The Santeria Church responded with suits against the city and, like the Amish, they lost their case at every step—except the last one.

On the Supreme Court bench, all the justices ruled in favor of Santeria. However, since the justices adopted varying grounds for finding in the church's favor, four separate opinions were offered. Justice Anthony Kennedy delivered the opinion of the Court, except for one specified part. Kennedy saw in the city's ordinances a deliberate attempt to suppress a religion. And government could not in a selective manner impose burdens on religiously motivated conduct. Adherence to this principle, said Kennedy, "is essential to the protection of the rights guaranteed by the Free Exercise Clause." All officials, he added, must be alert to even the "slightest suspicion" that their actions may be motivated by hostility toward a religion. "Legislators may not devise mechanisms," Kennedy concluded, "overt or disguised, designed to persecute or oppress a religion or its practices."

Justice Antonin Scalia, joined by Chief Justice William Rehnquist, preferred to concentrate on the effects of the Florida laws more than their purpose. Justice David Souter concurred in the Court's judgment "without reservation" but found some of the precedents cited by the Court to be troublesome and worthy of reconsideration. Justice Harry Blackmun, joined by Justice Sandra Day O'Connor, emphasized that the free exercise of religion "extends beyond those rare occasions on which government targets religion (or a particular religion) for disfavored treatment, as is done in this case."

With a boost from the Supreme Court, as well as with a growing acceptance of religious pluralism in the nation, Santeria flourished well beyond the borders of Florida. In New York City, for example, members who had worshiped in privacy if not secrecy since the 1940s began to take a more public stance. And membership grew to include middle-class professionals and members of diverse ethnic groups. Indeed, this once nearly invisible sect now appears on the Internet, distributes compact discs of its music, and will be featured in a projected Broadway musical.

No group in United States history has suffered longer or more unrelenting persecution than Native Americans. Not until 1924 did American Indians receive U.S. citizenship, and not until 1978 did Congress explicitly assure their religious freedom. On August 11, 1978, the U.S. Congress passed a joint resolution stating that it would be the policy of the United States to "protect and preserve for American Indians their inherent right of freedom to believe, express, and exercise" their traditional religions. This included, but was not limited to, access to sacred sites, "use and possession of sacred objects, and the freedom to worship through ceremonials and traditional rites."

Sixty years before, Oklahoma had granted a charter to the Native American Church. Christian in its basic orientation, this church maintained some native practices, including as a part of its regular ritual the use of peyote or mescal, a stimulant drug derived from a spineless cactus grown in Mexico and the southwestern United States. This practice caused the church to become unpopular in some areas and to encounter legal problems in others. The peyote ritual occupied center stage in the

Supreme Court's judgment rendered in 1990 (*Oregon Employment Division* v. *Smith*).

Two Klamuth Indians, Alfred Smith and Galen Black, were fired from their jobs because they had used peyote for sacramental purposes in a Native American Church ceremony. Both men were members of this church. When they applied for unemployment benefits, these were denied because of their "misconduct." They sought relief from the courts on the grounds that their free exercise of religion had been infringed. The Oregon Supreme Court agreed with the complaint of the two Native Americans, whereupon the Oregon Employment Division appealed to the U.S. Supreme Court.

In a 6-to-3 decision, the Supreme Court reversed the decision of the Oregon court, thereby denying any unemployment benefits to Smith and Black. Justice Scalia, writing for the majority, noted that the two men

Peyote has ritual uses in many Native American activities, such as this Big Moon ceremony in Delaware. The Supreme Court overturned the Oregon state court's decision to allow peyote consumption as part of a religious ritual.

violated an Oregon law making the use of peyote a criminal offense. "We have never held," Scalia wrote, "that an individual's religious beliefs excuse him from compliance with an otherwise valid law prohibiting conduct that the State is free to regulate." Moreover, the traditional appeal to a "compelling interest" as the only valid reason for a state to interfere with the free exercise of religion was neither necessary nor wise. "Any society adopting such a system would be courting anarchy," Scalia added, especially a society as religiously diverse as the United States. "We cannot afford the luxury," he declared, of treating laws as "presumptively invalid" in free-exercise cases just because a "compelling interest" cannot be demonstrated. To be sure, this might result in "a relative disadvantage" for those whose religious practices "are not widely engaged in." But, Scalia concluded, that was better than "a system in which each conscience is a law unto itself."

Chief Justice Rehnquist, as well as Justices White, Stevens, and Kennedy, joined in this opinion. Justice O'Connor agreed with the judgment reached but vigorously denounced the grounds on which it was based. Justices Brennan, Marshall, and Blackmun supported her objections but not her approval of the Court's judgment. Justice Blackmun wrote a separate dissenting opinion in which Brennan and Marshall joined.

O'Connor rejected Scalia's reasoning because it "dramatically departs from well-settled First Amendment jurisprudence." "If the First Amendment is to have any vitality," she argued, it cannot be held in reserve for some "extreme and hypothetical situation." The Court had previously always relied on the "compelling interest" test, she pointed out, for religious liberty occupies a "preferred position" and cannot be lightly brushed aside, especially where religious minorities are concerned. The First Amendment, O'Connor added, "was enacted precisely to protect the rights of those whose religious practices are not shared by the majority and may be viewed with hostility." She concluded by recalling the harsh effects that a simpleminded majority rule "has had on the unpopular or emerging religious groups such as the Jehovah's Witnesses and the Amish."

In 1942 Protestants in
Kentucky affirm their faith
by handling snakes during
a service. Government
often intervened to end
this "dangerous" practice,
testing the bounds of religious freedom.

The three dissenters, with Justice Blackmun as spokesman, vigorously objected to the new direction the Court had suddenly taken. In their view, the majority apparently agreed "that strict scrutiny of a state law burdening the free exercise of religion is a 'luxury' that a well-ordered society cannot afford." On the contrary, Blackmun protested, he did not believe "the Founders thought their dearly bought freedom from religious persecution a 'luxury,' but an essential element of liberty." Referring to the American Indian Religious Freedom Act passed in 1978, Blackmun declared that while it did not bestow new rights, it did require the Court to "scrupulously apply its free exercise analysis to the religious claims of Native Americans, however unorthodox they may be."

If the justices reacted strongly, those outside the Supreme Court reacted even more strongly. Public concerns about the fate of religious liberty echoed from one side of the country to the other. Religious groups protested that the free exercise of religion was in danger as never before.

And Congressional leaders within both parties registered their strong complaints as well. So serious and sustained were the objections that Congress in 1993 passed a Religious Freedom Restoration Act. The clear intent of this act was to undo the damage, as it was widely perceived, that the *Smith* decision had inflicted upon the First Amendment.

This act had the broadest support from U.S. religious communities. Protestants and Catholics joined with Jews and Muslims to urge its passage. Needless to say, the Native American Church also endorsed the measure. And its political support was equally broad: the House of Representatives passed it unanimously and the Senate by a vote of 97 to 3. When President Bill Clinton signed the bill on November 16, 1993, he observed that the Religious Freedom Restoration Act honored "the principle that our laws and institutions should not impede or hinder, but rather should protect and preserve fundamental religious liberties." For that moment, at least, the free-exercise clause of the First Amendment looked both healthy and secure.

But in 1997 (*Boerne* v. *P. F. Flores*) the Supreme Court, by a vote of 6 to 3, found the Religious Freedom Restoration Act to be unconstitutional. The case concerned the effort of a Roman Catholic church near San Antonio, Texas, to enlarge its sanctuary for worship. The city of Boerne denied the request on the grounds that the church was in a historic preservation district. At that point, the archbishop of San Antonio, Patrick Flores, sued the city for denying its religious freedom in violation of the provisions of the Religious Freedom Restoration Act. The case was somewhat muddied by questions of state versus federal rights, and even more by the issue of whether the U.S. Congress or the U.S. Supreme Court had the right to define the meaning of the free-exercise clause of the First Amendment.

Justice Kennedy, speaking for the Court's majority, explained that while Congress had the right to enforce violations of the Constitution, it did not have the power to determine what constituted such a violation. Moreover, Kennedy added, "Our national experience teaches that the Constitution is preserved best when each part of the government respects both the Constitution and the proper actions and determinations of

Religious Freedom Restoration Act, 1993

In 1997 the Supreme Court, by a vote of 6 to 3, declared this act to be unconstitutional.

Section 2. Congressional Findings and Declaration of Purposes

A. Findings. The Congress finds that—

1. the framers of the Constitution, recognizing free exercise of religion as an unalienable right, secured its protection in the First Amendment to the Constitution;

2. laws "neutral" toward religion may burden religious exercise as surely as laws intended to interfere with religious exercise;

3. governments should not burden religious exercise without compelling justification;

4. in *Employment Division* v. *Smith* (1990) the Supreme Court virtually eliminated the requirement that the government justify burdens on religious exercise imposed by laws neutral toward religion; and,

5. the compelling interest test as set forth in prior Federal court rulings is a workable test for striking sensible balances between religious liberty and competing prior governmental interests.

B. Purposes. The purposes of this Act are—

1. to restore the compelling interest test as set forth in *Sherbert* v. *Verner* (1963) and *Wisconsin* v. *Yoder* (1972) and to guarantee its application in all cases where free exercise of religion is burdened; and,

2. to provide a claim or defense to persons whose religious exercise is burdened by government.

A Muslim girl in a public school wears a headdress in observance of her faith. Subject to local controls, public schools have no consistent policy regarding religious clothing or other religious requirements.

the other branches." The Religious Freedom Restoration Act, in short, "contradicts vital principles necessary to maintain separation of powers and the federal balance."

The longest and strongest dissent came from the pen of Justice Sandra Day O'Connor, who argued vigorously that the 1990 *Smith* case was wrongly decided and should be reheard. "I believe that we should reexamine our holding in *Smith*," she noted. "In its place, I would return to a rule that requires government to justify any substantial burden on religiously motivated conduct by a compelling state interest and to impose that burden only by means narrowly tailored to achieve that interest."

The 1997 decision, O'Connor commented simply, "has harmed religious liberty." Many political and religious leaders agreed, as they searched for some other means to achieve their desired end of protecting the free exercise of religion. And religious minorities also watched with keen interest. Muslim schoolgirls, for example, are obliged to assert their right to wear religiously prescribed clothing. And during the monthlong fast known as Ramadan, all faithful Muslims refuse to eat or drink during the daylight hours. Some schools allow Muslim students to leave early on Fridays to attend the most important afternoon prayers of the week, but other schools do not. As the nation becomes increasingly pluralistic and as it becomes ever more obvious that one calendar does not fit all, the Supreme Court will no doubt be called upon repeatedly to help draw the lines that both define and preserve the free exercise of religion.

Chapter 8

The Supreme Court and the Road Ahead

998 U.S. Supreme
t. First row, seated, left
ht: Associate Justices
nin Scalia and John
Stevens, Chief Justice
m H. Rehnquist,
iate Justices Sandra
)'Connor, and Anthony
nnedy; back row,
ling, left to right:
iate Justices Ruth
r Ginsburg, David H.
er, Clarence Thomas,
tephen Breyer.

The Supreme Court is generally perceived as a relatively stable institition: that is, no elections every two or four years that bring in a flood of new faces, and no wholesale resignations are required when the political control of the White House or the Congress shifts. Each justice to this Court is appointed for life (barring any gross misconduct), and most justices serve far beyond such retirement milestones as age 65 or 70. Moreover, the Court endeavors, not always successfully, to avoid the passionate partisanship more readily evident in the legislative and executive branches of government. During the Presidential State of the Union address, for example, the members of the Court attend as a group, fully robed and seated in a prominent position. Unlike the members of Congress, who usually interrupt the President's speech with applause or even cheering, the justices maintain a sober demeanor throughout the President's speech.

In hearing the cases that come before them, on the other hand, the justices are neither silent nor united. They question the lawyers who represent the opposing sides, sometimes sharply, and interrupt them as often as individual temperament dictates. The public is allowed to view this part of the proceedings. After this "open court," however, discussion and deliberation among the justices themselves is carried on behind closed doors, with neither press nor public in attendance. Not until a decision is announced, typically several months later, does the public have another opportunity to observe the Court in action, as opinions are handed down and dissents registered. Across the land, newspapers report the results, some (such as the *New York Times*) in considerable detail. Within weeks, new issues of the official *U.S. Supreme Court Reports* reach libraries, law schools, and government document repositories.

All this activity takes place in accordance with strict rules and honored traditions. The black-robed formality may even suggest that the nine justices present a united front. Unanimity, however, notably in the recent church-state cases that we have examined, is often elusive. The justices avoid all party politics, but other kinds of partisanship divide them. To describe these divisions, the unsatisfactory labels of liberal or conservative or centrist are sometimes applied. And in religion, the equally unsatisfactory designations of accommodationist (favoring more cooperation between government and religion) or separationist (favoring less contact between the civil and ecclesiastical realms) may also be called upon as a convenient, if rarely precise, shorthand.

In 1995 the Supreme Court decided a case that arose from an institution founded by Thomas Jefferson: the University of Virginia. The question was whether this public university could decline to spend student-fee monies to support a magazine (*Wide Awake*) that advocated an evangelical Christian point of view. The university regarded the funding of such a periodical as a violation of the establishment clause of the First Amendment. The magazine staff, led by Ronald Rosenberger, protested that the denial of funds violated their freedom of speech and of press, their free exercise of religion, and the equal-protection provisions of federal and state constitutions. A district court and a federal appeals court supported the position of the University of Virginia. The U.S. Supreme Court, on the other hand, found in favor of the student magazine. It perhaps comes as no surprise to learn that the justices were divided 5 to 4.

Justice Anthony Kennedy wrote the majority opinion in *Ronald W. Rosenberger et al.* v. *Rector and Visitors of the University of Virginia et al.;* Justices Scalia, O'Connor, and Thomas, along with Chief Justice

vol. 6 no. 2

wide AWAKE

a Christian perspective at the university of virginia

UNIVERSITY OF VIRGINIA

The University of Virginia denied funding to *Wide Awake,* but the Supreme Court ruled the school's action violated the principle of neutrality.

Rehnquist, joined in his opinion. Kennedy argued that since the university supported many other student publications, to deny support to a religious one was to violate the principle of neutrality. As long as the distribution of funds was neutral and evenhanded, Kennedy explained, the establishment clause was not an issue. The object of the Student Activities Fund, he added, was "to open a forum for speech and to support various student enterprises, including the publication of newspapers, in recognition of the diversity and creativity of student life." Such a program did not favor religion, but neither did it discriminate against religion.

In weighing particularly the free speech aspect of the case, Justice Kennedy noted the dangers in granting the university the right to review the content of the student publications "to determine whether or not they are based on some ultimate idea." Such action would have a "chilling" effect on individual thought and expression. "That danger is especially real," he continued, "in a University setting, where the State acts against a background and tradition of thought and experiment that is at the center of our intellectual and philosophical tradition." If the university objects to writings dedicated to first principles, then the contributions of Karl Marx, Bertrand Russell, and others would have to be excluded from student publications. "Plato could contrive perhaps to submit an acceptable essay on making pasta or peanut butter cookies, provided he did not point out their (necessary) imperfections," Kennedy wrote.

On the other side of the argument, Justice David Souter (joined by Justices Stevens, Ginsburg, and Breyer) asserted that the establishment clause could not be so readily dismissed. Nor was free speech the primary constitutional question to consider. Rather, said Souter, the question was whether any agency of government could properly be in the business of subsidizing the kind of explicit evangelical activity that *Wide Awake* represented. Souter thought that the Court's majority had not paid sufficient attention to the content of the magazine—a magazine whose masthead contained the words of the apostle Paul: "The hour has come for you to awake from your slumber, because our salvation is nearer now than when we first believed. Romans 13:11."

A 1990 issue of *Wide Awake,* even more graphic in its call for slumberers to seek salvation, prompted Souter to quote at some length. "When you get to the final gate, the Lord will be handing out boarding passes, and He will examine your ticket," the magazine declared. "If, in your lifetime, you did not request a seat on His Friendly Skies Flyer by trusting Him and asking Him to be your pilot, then you will not be on his list of reserved seats (and the Lord will know you not).... You will be met by your chosen pilot and flown straight to Hell on an express jet (without air conditioning or toilets, of course)." This kind of writing, Souter noted, "is not the discourse of the scholar's study or the seminar room, but of the evangelist's mission station and the pulpit." Souter therefore concluded: "Using public funds for the direct subsidization of preaching the word is categorically forbidden under the Establishment Clause, and if the Clause was meant to accomplish nothing else, it was meant to bar this use of public money."

This case, which attracted wide attention, had its own intrinsic merit, of course. But it also revealed the continuing deep divisions in the Court. Indeed, these divisions, perhaps somewhat hardened, reappeared in 2001, with a shift from a 5 to 4 split to a 6 to 3 one. In *Good News Club* v. *Milford* [New York] *Central School,* the Court considered whether evangelistic activity could constitutionally take place on public school property after the regular school day ended at 3 p.m. While the Court had approved similar evangelism in the *Rosenberger* case, the activity in that instance pertained only to university students. *Good News Club,* by contrast, concerned students from kindergarten through sixth grade. Would that difference in age level alter the judgment?

For the six-person majority, it did not. Writing for that majority, Justice Clarence Thomas explained that the basic issue in both cases was free speech. And it was wholly inappropriate, he declared, to discriminate against one particular form of speech: namely, religious speech. In taking this stance, he added, the Court did not threaten neutrality, but ensured it. The three dissenters, on the contrary, pointed out that the Good News Club was part of a national organization whose stated purpose was to "evangelize boys and girls with the Gospel of the Lord Jesus Christ." The club's dominant purpose, therefore, was neither instruction nor discussion, but conversion. And that, in the view of the dissenters, was constitutionally impermissible and potentially divisive within the Milford community.

If the judicial branch of the U.S. government was kept busy in the religious arena, the legislative branch was not idle, either. Ever since the Court's decisions on prayer in the 1960s, many congressional leaders have proposed amending the Constitution in order to allow official prayers in the public schools. So far, Congress has not yet been able to muster the necessary two-thirds vote needed to pass an amendment; were Congress able to do so, that amendment would still have to be approved by three-

The U.S. Congress recites the Pledge of Allegiance, which includes the words "under God," at Federal Hall in New York City. As a tribute to the victims of the September 11, 2001, tragedy they met a year in this historic landmark, site of the First Congress.

fourths of the states. This is a cumbersome and difficult process, deliberately made so by the framers of the Constitution.

In the 1990s various Congressmen drew up somewhat broader amendments, these aimed to protect (in the words of one version) the rights of public school students to acknowledge "the religious heritage, beliefs, or traditions of the people" and to engage in "student-sponsored prayer in public schools." By 1997, the House and Senate had agreed on a single version, called the Religious Freedom Amendment. When this Amendment came to the floor of the House for a vote in 1998, it passed (224 to 203), but not by the necessary two-thirds margin. However, in 2000 a more restricted bill—not an amendment—did pass into law; it bore the burdensome title of the Religious Land Use and Institutionalized Persons Act. By the terms of this law, local zoning requirements could not be used against churches unless a "compelling interest" could be clearly established.

Another portion of the law sought to protect prisoners in the practice of their religion, though prison officials did not have to grant requests that would undermine the institution's discipline, order, and security.

Much of the argument on these questions revolves around the matter of how much religion in the nation's public life is permissible or desirable. That issue soared to new heights in 2002 when a federal judge, Alfred Goodwin of the Court of Appeals for the Ninth Circuit, ruled that the phrase "under God" in the pledge of allegiance was unconstitutional. "A profession that we are a nation 'under God,'" he wrote, "is identical, for Establishment Clause purposes, to a profession that we are a nation 'under Jesus,' a nation 'under Vishnu,' a nation 'under Zeus,' or a nation 'under no god.'" His decision provoked a national outcry so great that Judge Goodwin himself blocked the implementation of his order until the full Ninth Circuit Court could hear the case or—if it came to that—the Supreme Court could hear and decide the case. Congress responded immediately by showing up the next day for the ritual pledge of allegiance in record numbers, reciting it with special vocal emphasis on the "under God." Meanwhile, the American public learned, many for the first time, that this phrase had been added only in 1954, at the height of the Cold War against Soviet communism. The original pledge, written in 1892 by a former Baptist clergyman, was intended to promote national unity regardless of race, creed, or ethnic background.

And national unity seemed indeed to be the issue, as it had been in flag-saluting or flag-burning, in bible reading or bible spurning, in Presidential calls for prayer and fasting or Presidential deference to religious leaders for these ceremonies. The commotion over the pledge of allegiance led on the part of some Americans to a "Where will it all end?" reaction, while to others it seemed like an appropriate place to start ridding the nation of other vestiges of what Justice William Brennan once called "ceremonial deism." At Presidential inaugurations, for example, religious leaders offer prayers, the President takes his oath of office with his hand on the bible (the King James Version regularly, except for John F. Kennedy's use of the family Catholic bible), and the President concludes his oath with the traditional phrase—inserted by George Washington—

"So help me God." Most courts also employ that phrase in swearing in a witness, even as they utilize the bible once again.

Then there is the motto "In God We Trust" imprinted on our coins and bills. Early in the twentieth century President Theodore Roosevelt, in ordering new money designs, directed that this motto be dropped, since no law required it. Congress immediately responded by passing a law requiring the motto on American money, so "In God We Trust" remains. Roosevelt's motive was not anti-religious, but quite the contrary. He thought that this common use trivialized religion, making it a "constant source of jest and ridicule." But many others, of course, see in the omnipresence of these words a comforting affirmation of a national faith. The courts have not spoken to this issue and, since one must prove some injury or harm before taking his or her case to court, this instance of "ceremonial deism" may well endure.

While Congress and the courts struggle to define lines between church and state, the executive branch under President George W. Bush has proposed faith-based initiatives or "charitable choice" that would permit federal subsidies for the charitable activities of religious groups. Though this program received fairly wide endorsement initially, its problems loom larger and larger. Faith-based organizations, for one thing, seek to limit their employees to members of their own religious communities. Some members of Congress who were initially supportive of the Bush policy lost enthusiasm when they learned that denominations of which they did not approve would also be included in the federal grants. More fundamentally, many churches grew anxious about their own independence if they accepted large amounts of governmental money. Would they become tools instead of critics of the federal establishment? Other citizens grew anxious about the constitutionality of the entire effort that builds connections instead of barriers between the ecclesiastical and the civil realms. In 2002, the U.S. Department of Labor awarded its first grants under this Presidential initiative. Even so, it appears that federal financing of faith-based organizations will move slowly. In pressing their several ways through the murky landscape of church-state relations, the judicial, legislative, and executive branches all search for clear and guiding lights.

Sometimes the church-state cases reviewed here may look puny and barely worth worrying about: a 10-cent bus fare in New Jersey, a 50-cent peddling permit in Connecticut, a $5.40 annual tax bill in New York, a parade permit here, a schoolbook there. But James Madison noted that the Bostonians' refusal in 1774 to pay a threepenny-a-pound tax on tea was also just a piddling amount. Yet "the people of the U.S. owe their independence and their liberty," Madison wrote, "to the wisdom of descrying [discerning] in the minute Tax . . . the magnitude of the evil comprised in the precedent." To adapt a line from Michelangelo, religious liberty is made up of a series of trifles, but religious liberty is no trifle.

Chronology

1619
Legal establishment of the
Anglican Church in Virginia

1630
Congregationalism is launched in
Massachusetts Bay Colony

1636
Roger Williams, banished by the
General Court of Massachusetts,
founds Rhode Island, a colony
in which church and state are
separate

1644
Publication (in England) of
Roger Williams's *Bloudy Tenant
of Persecution*

1649
Maryland Assembly passes Act of
Toleration

1659–61
Four Quakers hanged on Boston
Common

1670
Publication (in England) of
William Penn's *Great Case of
Liberty of Conscience*

1689
Act of Toleration passed in
England

1776–83
American Revolution secures civil
and ecclesiastical liberty

1776
Process of disestablishing the Anglican Church in Virginia begins

1786
Virginia legislature passes Thomas
Jefferson's Bill for Establishing
Religious Freedom

1788
U.S. Constitution is ratified

1791
Ratification of the Bill of Rights (first
10 amendments to the Constitution)

1815
Supreme Court rules on the posses-
sion of glebe lands by the Episcopal
Church after disestablishment in
Virginia (*Terret* v. *Taylor*)

1818
Congregational Church is disestablished in Connecticut

1819
Supreme Court renders decision
that protects the role of churches in
the founding of denominational
colleges (*Dartmouth College* v.
Woodward)

1833

Congregational Church is disestablished in Massachusetts

1854

Know-Nothing (or American) party organizes to keep Catholics (and others) from public office

1865

Congress sanctions the presence of the phrase "In God We Trust" on certain gold and silver coins

1868

Congress ratifies the Fourteenth Amendment

1872

Supreme Court hears first case of internal church controversy (*Watson* v. *Jones*)

1879–90

U.S. Supreme Court hears "Mormon cases" (*Reynolds* v. *United States, Davis* v. *Beason*)

1884

Catholic bishops in the United States call for a comprehensive parochial school system

1925

Scopes trial held in Dayton, Tennessee; Supreme Court recognizes parental right to send children to parochial or private schools

1940

Free-exercise clause of the First Amendment is applied to the states; Supreme Court hears first of many Jehovah's Witnesses cases (*Cantwell* v. *Connecticut*)

1947

Religious establishment clause of the First Amendment is applied to the states; Supreme Court hears first post–World War II case involving private education

1961–63

Several Sunday law cases reach Supreme Court (*Braunfeld* v. *Brown, Gallagher* v. *Crown Kosher Super Market*)

1962–63

Supreme Court decides cases dealing with prayer and Bible reading in the public schools (*Engel* v. *Vitale*)

1965

In *Griswold* v. *Connecticut* Supreme Court nullifies a state law that prohibited birth control practices by married couples

1965–71

Supreme Court hears cases concerning conscientious objection to military service (*U.S.* v. *Seeger*)

1970

Supreme Court decides question of tax exemption for churches and synagogues (*Walz* v. *Tax Commission of the City of New York*)

1971

Supreme Court rules on issues of federal salary supplements to non-public school teacher's salaries (*Lemon* v. *Kurtzman, Earley* v. *DiCenso*)

1972

Supreme Court exempts Amish children from state compulsory education laws (*Wisconsin* v. *Yoder*)

By a vote of 7 to 2, Supreme Court in *Roe* v. *Wade* hands down a major ruling on abortion

1973

Supreme Court rules on issues of tuition grants and tax credits for private school students (*PEARL* v. *Nyquist*)

1975

Pennsylvania case reveals difficulties and complexities of federal aid to private education

1984

Federal government establishes full diplomatic relations with the Vatican; Supreme Court is split over issues of public funding for religious displays (*Lynch* v. *Donnelly*)

1987

Creationism versus Darwinism is the focus of a Louisiana case decided by the Supreme Court (*Edwards* v. *Aguillard*)

In a case out of Missouri (*Webster* v. *Reproductive Services*), Supreme Court narrowly sustains *Roe* v. *Wade*

1990

Supreme Court relaxes "compelling interest" test for placing a limitation on religious liberty (*Oregon Employment Division* v. *Smith*)

1992

In a flurry of divided opinions, Supreme Court (in *Planned Parenthood* v. *Casey*) once more keeps *Roe* v. *Wade* alive

1993

Congress passes Religious Freedom Restoration Act

1994

Supreme Court invalidates a school district drawn to accommodate a sect of Hasidic Jews (*Board of Education of Kiryas Joel Village School District* v. *Louis Grunet et al.*)

1995

A divided Supreme Court rules on a University of Virginia case involving student publication that promoted religious views (*Ronald W. Rosenberger et al.* v. *Rector and Visitors of the University of Virginia et al.*)

1997

Supreme Court declares Religious Freedom Restoration Act unconstitutional (*Boerne* v. *P. F. Flores*)

2000

A Louisiana case gives the Supreme Court (in a 6 to 3 vote) an opportunity to expand aid to parochial school (*Mitchell* v. *Helms*)

In *Santa Fe Independent School District* v. *Doe,* the Court (6 to 3) rules school prayers before football games to be unconstitutional

2001

By another 6 to 3 vote, but with different sides, Supreme Court approves evangelistic activity among younger children on public school grounds (*Good News Club* v. *Milford Central School*)

2002

After a long absence from Jehovah's Witnesses cases, Supreme Court (8 to 1) finds that a municipal permit requirement is unconstitutional

By a narrow margin of 5 to 4, Supreme Court affirms the constitutionality of a voucher program out of Ohio (*Zelman* v. *Simmons-Harris*)

A federal judge in California declares the "under God" language in the pledge of allegiance to be unconstitutional; by a vote of 90 to 0, the U.S. Senate reaffirms the text of the pledge of allegiance in its present form

Further Reading

GENERAL READING ON RELIGION IN THE UNITED STATES

Albanese, Catherine. *America: Religions and Religion*. 3rd edition. Belmont, Calif.: Wadsworth, 1999.

Butler, Jon, and Harry S. Stout, eds. *Religion in American History: A Reader*. New York: Oxford University Press, 1997.

Gaustad, Edwin S. and Leigh E. Schmidt. *The Religious History of America*. San Francisco: Harper San Francisco, 2002.

Marty, Martin. *Pilgrims in Their Own Land*. New York: Penguin, 1985.

Williams, Peter. *American Religions: From Their Origins to the Twenty-first Century*. Urbana: University of Illinois Press, 2002.

COLONIAL AND EARLY NATIONAL PERIODS

Buckley, Thomas E., S.J. *Church and State in Revolutionary Virginia, 1776–1787*. Charlottesville: University Press of Virginia, 1977.

Curry, Thomas J. *The First Freedoms: Church and State and the Passing of the First Amendment*. New York: Oxford University Press, 1986.

Davis, Derek H. *Religion and the Continental Congress, 1774–1789: Contributions to Original Intent*. New York: Oxford University Press, 2000.

Gaustad, Edwin S. *Roger Williams: Prophet of Liberty*. New York: Oxford University Press, 2001.

———. *Sworn on the Altar of God: A Religious Biography of Thomas Jefferson*. Grand Rapids, Mich.: Eerdmans, 1996.

Hutson, James H. *Religion and the Founding of the American Republic*. Washington, D.C.: Library of Congress, 1998.

McLoughlin, William G. *New England Dissent, 1630–1833: The Baptists and the Separation of Church and State*. 2 vols. Cambridge: Harvard University Press, 1971.

Miller, William Lee. *The First Liberty: Religion and the American Republic.* New York: Knopf, 1986.

COMMENTARY ON RELIGIOUS LIBERTY IN THE UNITED STATES

Curry, Thomas J. *Farewell to Christendom: The Future of Church and State in America.* New York: Oxford University Press, 2001.

Davis, Derek H. *The Separation of Church and State Defended: Selected Writings of James E. Wood, Jr.* Waco, Tex.: J. M. Dawson Institute, 1995.

Driesbach, Daniel L. *Real Threat and Mere Shadow: Religious Liberty and the First Amendment.* Westchester, Ill.: Crossway, 1987.

Fraser, James W. *Between Church and State: Religion and Public Education in a Multicultural America, 1600–2000.* New York: St. Martin's, 1999.

Gartner, Lloyd P., ed. *Jewish Education in the United States: A Documentary History.* New York: Teachers College, 1969.

Gordon, Sarah B. *The Mormon Question: Polygamy and Constitutional Conflict in 19th Century America.* Chapel Hill: University of North Carolina Press, 2002.

Hamburger, Philip. *Separation of Church and State.* Cambridge: Harvard University Press, 2002.

Hull, N. E. H. and Hoffer, P. C. *Roe v. Wade: The Abortion Rights Controversy in American History.* Lawrence: University Press of Kansas, 2001.

Larson, Edward J. *Trial and Error: The American Controversy Over Creation and Evolution.* Cambridge, Mass.: MIT Press, 1983.

McCluskey, Neil G. *Catholic Education in America: A Documentary History.* Garden City, N.Y.: Doubleday, 1969.

McMillan, Richard C. *Religion in the Public Schools: An Introduction.* Macon, Ga.: Mercer University Press, 1983.

Noonan, John T., Jr. *The Lustre of Our Country: The American Experience of Religious Freedom.* Berkeley: University of California Press, 1998.

Sorauf, Frank J. *The Wall of Separation: The Constitutional Politics of Church and State.* Princeton, N.J.: Princeton University Press, 1976.

Thiemann, Ronald F. *Religion in Public Life: A Dilemma for Democracy.* Washington, D.C.: Georgetown University Press, 1996.

Witte, John, Jr. *Religion and the American Constitutional Experiment.* Boulder, Colo.: Westview Press, 2000.

SUPREME COURT DECISIONS

The principal source for church-state questions in the contemporary United States is the Supreme Court's own decisions. If your community has a law library or a library that serves as a government repository, you should have access to the U.S. Supreme Court Reports, issued frequently throughout the year and then bound together in annual volumes. If you have the name of the case (for example, *Meek* v. *Pittenger*) that you are researching and the year that it was decided, the librarian should be able to help you find the complete text of the decision, along with the dissents.

The internet also provides easy access to Supreme Court decisions. Although the U.S. Supreme Court does not currently maintain an official website with case information, it does recommend the following open access sites: *www.Cornell.law.edu* and *www.findlaw.com*. As an alternative to these options, consider the two anthologies noted below.

Alley, Robert S., ed. *The Supreme Court on Church and State.* New York: Oxford University Press, 1988.

Miller, Robert T., and Ronald B. Flowers, eds. *Toward Benevolent Neutrality: Church, State, and the Supreme Court.* 5th edition. Waco, Tex.: Baylor University Press, 1996.

BIBLIOGRAPHY

Wilson, John F., ed. *Church and State in America: A Bibliographical Guide.* 2 vols. Westport, Conn.: Greenwood, 1986–87. This work, extending from the colonial period through the late 20th century, offers ample guidance for virtually any church-state topic that one might wish to pursue.

Index

Picture Credits

Americans United for the Separation of Church and State: 67; AP/Wide World Photos: 136; Archdiocese of Boston Archives: 114; Architect of the Capitol: 20; Archive Photos: 103; Courtesy the Billy Graham Center Museum: 34, 49; Brigham Young University: 121; Chicago Historical Society: 56; © The Church of Jesus Christ of Latter-day Saints, Courtesy of LDS Historical Dept., Archives: 58; Courtesy Commonwealth of Massachusetts: 14, 21, 23, 89; Fareed Numan/Muslim American Exhibition Project: 148; Gary Tong: 48; General Conference of Seventh-day Adventists: 135; Eustacio Humphrey © 2002 *The Plain Dealer*. All rights reserved. Reprinted with permission: 122; Independence National Historic Park: 43; Library of Congress: 6, 13, 17, 25, 32, 33, 44, 46, 50, 52, 53, 57, 86, 88, 106; Maryland State Archives: 26; Massachusetts Historical Society: 30; Josh Mathes, Collection of the Supreme Court of the United States: 10; Bruce McClelland, *The Arizona Daily Star*: 118; National Archives: 64, 145; National Catholic Education Association: 112, 116; Courtesy National Museum of the American Indian, Smithsonian Institution: 142; New Horizon School, Pasadena, California: 108; Collection of the New-York Historical Society: 35; Pacific Press: 68; Dale Omori © 2002 *The Plain Dealer*. All rights reserved. Reprinted by permission: 130; Courtesy, Peabody Essex Museum, Salem, MA: 24; Pool/Reuters/Timepix: 156; Presbyterian Church (USA): 18; © Providence Journal Bulletin: 81, 100; Reuters (Gary A. Cameron/Archive Photos): 139; Reuters (Susan Greenwood/Archive Photos): 140; Peter F. Rothermel, "Patrick Henry Before the House of Burgesses, "Red Hill-Patrick Henry National Memorial: 37; Southern Baptist Historical Library and Archives, Nashville, Tennessee: 104; Cecil Stoughton, LBJ Library Collection: 2; Collection of the Supreme Court of the United States: 54, 90; Collection of the Supreme Court Historical Society: 150; Ira N. Toff: 135; United States Army Signal Corps: 82; UPI/Corbis-Bettman: 71, 94, 96, 98, 118, 126, 128, 131; Utah State Historical Society: 59; UVA/Wide Awake: 153; Westminster John Knox Press: 84; Taro Yamasaki/Timepix: 76

Text Credits

The sidebars in the Religion in American Life series contain extracts of historic documents. Source information on sidebars in this volume is as follows:

"The Quakers and Mary Dyer," p. 22–23: Horacial Rodgers, *Mary Dyer of Rhode Island* (Providence, R.I.: Preston M. Rounds, 1896).

"Thomas Jefferson's Statute for Establishing Religious Freedom," p. 40: Thomas Jefferson, *Notes on the State of Virginia* (Chapel Hill: University of North Carolina, 1982).

"Supreme Court Decision: *Davis v. Beason,*" p. 63: Davis v. Beason, 133 U.S. 333 (1890).

"Supreme Court Decision: *Lynch v. Donnelly,*" p. 78: Lynch v. Donnelly, 465 U.S. 668 (1984).

"Prayer and the U.S. Constitution," p. 99: Senate Joint Resolution 199, 97th Congress, second session.

"The Necessity for Parochial Schools," p. 110: Peter Guilday, ed., *The National Pastorals of the American Hierarchy, 1792–1919* (Washington: National Catholic Welfare Conference, 1923).

"Religious Freedom Restoration Act, 1993," p. 147: Public Law 103–141.

Edwin S. Gaustad

Edwin S. Gaustad is emeritus professor of history at the University of California, Riverside. He is the coauthor, with Philip L. Barlow, of *The New Historical Atlas of Religion in America*, which was named an Outstanding Reference Source of the Year by the American Library Association, and the author of numerous books on religious history, including *Neither King nor Prelate: Religion and the New Nation, Sworn on the Altar of God: A Religious Biography of Thomas Jefferson, A Documentary History of Religion in America (2 vols.), Liberty of Conscience: Roger Williams in America*, and with Leigh Schmidt, *The Religious History of America*.

Jon Butler

Jon Butler is the William Robertson Coe Professor of American Studies and History and Professor of Religious Studies at Yale University. He received his B.A. and Ph.D. in history from the University of Minnesota. He is the coauthor, with Harry S. Stout, of *Religion in American History: A Reader*, and the author of several other books on American religious history including *Awash in a Sea of Faith: Christianizing the American People*, which won the Beveridge Award for the best book in American history in 1990 from the American Historical Association.

Harry S. Stout

Harry S. Stout is the Jonathan Edwards Professor of American Christianity at Yale University. He is the general editor of the Religion in America series for Oxford University Press and co-editor of *Readings in American Religious History, New Directions in American Religious History, A Jonathan Edwards Reader*, and *The Dictionary of Christianity in America*. His book *The Divine Dramatist: George Whitefield and the Rise of Modern Evangelicalism* was nominated for a Pulitzer Prize in 1991.